The Funniest People in Movies: 250 Anecdotes

David Bruce

Published by David Bruce, 2022.

Table of Contents

***

All anecdotes have been retold in my own words to avoid plagiarism.

Anecdotes are usually short humorous stories. Sometimes they are thought-provoking or informative, not amusing.

DEDICATED TO MY SISTER ROSA

The Doing of Good Deeds is Important

As a free person, you can choose to live your life as a good person or as a bad person. To be a good person, do good deeds. To be a bad person, do bad deeds. If you do good deeds, you will become good. If you do bad deeds, you will become bad. To become the person you want to be, act as if you already are that kind of person. Each of us chooses what kind of person we will become. To become a good person, do the things a good person does. To become a bad person, do the things a bad person does. The opportunity to take action to become the kind of person you want to be is yours.

"I Will Go with You Into the Grave"

In a medieval Christian mystery play, a man asks who will go with him into the grave when he dies and give him support at the Day of Judgment. Time after time, he hears the answer, "I won't go with you into the grave." His wife won't go with him into the grave, his children won't go with him into the grave, his priest won't go with him into the grave, his friends won't go with him into the grave — even his wealth won't go with him into the grave. Finally, the man's good deeds say, "I will go with you into the grave," and the man and his good deeds knock at the door of death, together. Your good deeds will plead for you on the Day of Judgment.

"Do Small Kindnesses for People"

Amy Alkon, aka "The Advice Goddess," does good deeds, and she used to write an advice column for alternative newspapers. She advises, "Do small kindnesses for people." For example, she buys and reads a newspaper every day. When she is finished reading it, she will look around wherever she is — often, she is in a café — and often see somebody who is looking for a newspaper. She will then ask, "Sir, would you like my newspaper?" She points out, "You've noticed a stranger, you've solved their problem, you've gone out of your way to do it, and they're gonna feel very good about that, and I think people will tend to pass on good deeds, do other good deeds, if you do good deeds for them." She adds that "it does make a difference."

"Dear"

One of the things that Kurt Vonnegut, Jr., believes firmly is this: "God d*mn it, you've got to be kind." One of the things that cheers him up is buying a morning cup of coffee in New York City, which he describes as mad for money. He says, "You can go into a little café and the waitress calls you 'dear' even though she knows the bill will be a small expenditure and the tip tiny. So she is responding to you as a person and feels happy and wants to communicate."

Show the Haters that They are Wrong

Robert DeMott and Dave Smith became friends in the early 1970s. They had a number of things in common that facilitated their friendship: They were or would become editors, scholars, teachers, and writers, plus both had been told as undergraduates by professors that they "were not smart enough or able enough to amount to much in the 'real' world" — predictions that they ignored. Mr. DeMott became a noted John Steinbeck scholar, and Mr. Smith became a noted poet.

"The Touchstone For What Good Deeds Became In My Life"

Donna Delfino Dugay of Harper Woods, Michigan, grew up in California, where her family had a picnic at the beach when she was 11 years old. Her mother fixed each of the children a plate of fried chicken and potato salad, and then, Donna says, "When I looked up from my plate, my mother was fixing one more plate .... She turned away from us and walked over maybe 20 or 30 feet to where there was a man by himself. And he was picking his way through the trashcan. And my mother — I don't know whether she just put the plate there or whether she touched him gently or whether she said a few words — but I remember him turning to her in a gesture of thankfulness." Years later, when Donna asked her mother about this good deed, her mother claimed not to remember it; however, Donna says, "But for me, I remember it very well because for me, it was the touchstone for what good deeds became in my life."

"What is Hateful to Yourself, Do Not to Your Fellow Man"

A cart driver asked Rabbi Akiba to teach him the whole of the Torah all at once. Rabbi Akiba told him that Moses had stayed on the mountaintop 40 days and 40 nights to learn the Torah, but that if he really wanted to learn the basic principle of the Torah, he should learn this: "What is hateful to yourself, do not to your fellow man." Soon after, the cart driver went on a journey with two other men. They came to a field filled with seed pods, and the two other men took two seed pods each, but the cart driver took none. Then they came to a field filled with cabbages, and the two other men took two cabbages each, but the cart driver took none. They asked the cart driver why he wasn't taking anything, and he replied, "Thus did Rabbi Akiba teach me: 'What is hateful to yourself, do not to your fellow man.'"

Chapter 1: From Academy Awards to Alcohol

Academy Awards

• Oprah Winfrey was nominated for a Best Supporting Actress Oscar for her performance in her first feature film, *The Color Purple*, directed by Stephen Spielberg. Her father made sure that he saw the movie — it was the first time he had gone to a movie theater in 25 years. At the Academy Awards ceremony, Ms. Winfrey did not win, but she joked that she was relieved because her recently altered dress turned out to be too tight: "Perhaps God was saying to me, 'Oprah, you are not winning because your dress is too tight for you to make it up all those steps to receive the statuette.'"[1]

• In 1988, Jodie Foster won a Best Actress Oscar for her performance in *The Accused*. Following her acceptance speech, she joked backstage that she would immediately put the Oscar to good use: "I rented three videos last night ... and they said if I brought this in I would get them free."[2]

• When a man streaked across the stage during the Academy Awards, Oscar presenter David Niven said, "Let's not pay any attention to him. All he is doing is showing his shortcomings."[3]

Actors

• Javier Bardem, the Spanish actor who played the very evil murderer in the Coen Brothers' *No Country for Old Men*, had a number of other jobs before becoming an actor. In fact, for one day when he was a teenager, he was a stripper. He says, "Unfortunately, I made the mistake of talking about it years later and my mother and sister read the article. You talk about showing your *ss and then your mother reads all about it." As a citizen of Spain, he has a perspective different from that of Americans. For example, one day he had a nude scene, and the American crew made sure that he was covered up when he was not actually working — he definitely got the idea that people did not want to see his rear end. However, when he was murdering people in a scene, the Americans on set were happy. Mr. Bardem says that "the day I was killing people they were like, 'Yaah! That was good!' I know I don't have a nice *ss, but I would go for an *ss over killing people every time." A final difference between Spain and other countries — which in the opinion of the author of the book you are reading now definitely includes the USA — is this, according to Mr. Bardem, "I like the way people behave in my country. It's about being open to life instead of being obsessed about getting somewhere. There's a moment when they put the worries about paying the bills to one side and just live. In some countries, it's all about being number one, and if you are second you are a failure."[4]

• Kathy Bates won the Oscar for Best Actress in *Misery*, co-starring James Caan and made into a movie from a book by Stephen King. Director Rob Reiner told her that she had the lead part of Annie Wilkes, and Ms. Bates, who had never had the lead in a movie before, said, "The part. I've got it?" Mr. Reiner nodded and said, "You've got it." Unbelieving, Ms. Bates said, "The Annie part. Annie Wilkes. That part?" Mr. Reiner nodded again. Still unbelieving, Ms. Bates said, "Annie Wilkes. The lead. And I've got it and it's all set and everything?" Mr. Reiner replied, "All set." Ms. Bates said, "Let me just get this straight — I am playing Annie Wilkes, the lead, in *Misery*?" Again, Mr. Reiner replied affirmatively. Ms. Bates said, "It's done and everything, I mean, I am definitely playing Annie, and that's set and done and everything, no mistakes or anything?" Mr. Reiner said, "It is so set you wouldn't believe it." Ms. Bates sat silently for a moment and then asked, "Can I tell my mother?"[5]

• Jack Pierce was a master of makeup, and he created the makeup for such movie monsters as Frankenstein's Monster and the Wolf Man. When making up actor Boris Karloff as Frankenstein's Monster, Mr. Pierce made sure that the mask he had created came down only as far as Mr. Karloff's eyebrows. That way, the actor could use his eyes and mouth to express emotion. In the three movies starring Mr. Karloff as the monster, he moves very awkwardly — the result of having a heavy rod placed along his spine, and of wearing boots that together weighed 26 pounds. Mr. Karloff's performance as Frankenstein's Monster was very sympathetic and thousands of children wrote to him and showed compassion for the monster. Mr. Karloff remarked, "These children saw beyond the makeup and really understood."[6]

• Some people know what they like very early in their life. When Honor Blackman was 15 years old, her father let her choose which of two presents she wanted to receive: a bicycle or lessons in elocution. Young Honor, later to become the female lead in the movie *Goldfinger* and one of the female leads in the British TV cult classic *The Avengers*, chose the elocution lessons. (Another thing she likes is anecdotes. She tells about a young, overly enthusiastic director explaining the fine points of direction to actress Irene Handl, who listened patiently for a while, grew bored, and eventually told him, "Excuse me, I think you've mistaken me for someone who gives a f**k.")[7]

• In Quentin Tarantino's first film, the hit *Reservoir Dogs*, Kirk Baltz played a rookie police officer who is tortured by the sadistic Mr. Blonde, played by Michael Madsen. To get into character, Mr. Baltz asked Mr. Madsen to put him in the trunk of his car, then drive him around for five minutes. (In the movie, the police officer is put in the trunk of Mr. Blonde's car, then driven around.) Unfortunately for Mr. Baltz, Mr. Madsen also wanted to get into character. Acting like the sadistic Mr. Blonde, Mr. Madsen drove Mr. Baltz around for not five minutes, but for 45 minutes.[8]

• In Spike Lee's movie *Jungle Fever*, the beautiful Halle Berry plays a crack addict, a role she wanted because too many people assume that beautiful people don't get addicted to crack — or so the people casting this kind of role seem to think. She worked hard to prepare for the role. She asked co-star Samuel L. Jackson to drive her around some of New York City's poorest neighborhoods. She also visited a crack house in the presence of some police officers — who made her wear a bulletproof vest. Finally, for the 10 days before filming started, she did not take a bath.[9]

• In the screwball classic movie *It Happened One Night* is a famous scene in which Clark Gable and Claudette Colbert are hitchhiking, but they can't get a lift until Ms. Colbert shows her legs by the side of the road. At first, Ms. Colbert was shy and declined to show her legs in the scene, so director Frank Capra brought in a chorus girl to serve as Ms. Colbert's body double. Ms. Colbert looked at the chorus girl's pudgy legs, realized that movie-goers would think that the pudgy legs belonged to her, and decided to show her own thin and shapely legs in the scene.[10]

• Joe E. Brown was a wide-mouthed comedian who was featured in such films as *A Midsummer Night's Dream*, *Showboat*, and *Some Like It Hot*. For one movie, the hard-working comedian had to dive into a shallow lake. His director, Mervyn LeRoy, warned him that the lake was shallower than it looked, but when Mr. Brown came up after a dive that went too deep, his face was bloody. Mr. LeRoy wrote in his autobiography, "I passed out — I never could stand the sight of blood — but he just mopped it off and got ready for the next shot. He was a wonder."[11]

• As a writer, H. Allen Smith felt that he should not regard actors as being entirely human — it only encourages them. Therefore, despite being secretly thrilled when he met one of the celebrities of his day, he frequently did his best to show actors that they were nothing special. While working on a Hollywood movie studio lot, Basil Rathbone dressed in a costume such as one of the three Musketeers might wear: sword, very high boots, feathered cap, long cape, etc. Mr. Smith looked at Mr. Rathbone and asked, "You in pictures?"[12]

• Craig Russell, a Canadian female impersonator of genius, wrote and starred in the cult classic movie *Outrageous*. When the film was shown at the Virgin Islands Film Festival, Mr. Russell had the pleasure of winning awards for both Best Actor and Best Actress. A comedian, Mr. Russell used to say, "I'm a drag queen. I'm a transvestite. I'm a drug addict. I'm an alcoholic. I'm a homosexual. Other than that, I'm perfectly normal." He died of AIDS at the age of 42 on Oct. 30, 1990. [13]

• In the movie *Marathon Man*, a character played by Dustin Hoffman is tortured by a character played by Sir Laurence Olivier. On the day the torture scene was to be shot, Mr. Hoffman showed up looking very, very bad. He explained that to get ready to shoot the scene, he had stayed up two days and two nights without any sleep. Sir Laurence smiled, then said to Mr. Hoffman, "Why don't you just try acting? It's so much easier."[14]

• While housesitting for a friend, author Boze Hadleigh interviewed Cary Grant. That evening, the owner of the house came back. The telephone rang, and Mr. Hadleigh went to another room to answer it. When he returned, the owner of the house asked, "Who was that?" Mr. Hadleigh replied, "It was Cary Grant." The owner of the house laughed, although she was sitting in the armchair Mr. Grant had sat in earlier that day.[15]

• Whoopi Goldberg's first movie appearance was in *The Color Purple*, directed by Stephen Spielberg. Ms. Goldberg wanted to play the part of Sofia, but Mr. Spielberg offered her the bigger part of Celie. At first, Ms. Goldberg hesitated to accept the part, then she remembered that this was the great director Stephen Spielberg offering her an important part, and she told herself, "Wake up, stupid. Say yes." [16]

• The three Marx Brothers were such wild and crazy people in real life that movie directors had a hard time controlling them — they were always wandering off the set to place bets or to chase skirts. Finally, their directors were forced to lock up the Marx Brothers in cages on the set — they were released only when it was time for them to do a scene. (Chico had a telephone installed in his cage so he could call his bookie.)[17]

• John Huston directed *The Misfits*, the final film of both Clark Gable and Marilyn Monroe. During filming, Ms. Monroe became very ill, and Mr. Huston made her go to a hospital to recuperate. Later, a reporter asked why he had done that — was it out of consideration for the movie picture or out of consideration for Ms. Monroe? Mr. Huston replied, "The *picture*? The hell with the picture! The girl's whole *career* was at stake!"[18]

• While making the movie *The Heroes*, Terry-Thomas engaged in a bit of fun at Rod Steiger's expense. In the movie, Mr. Steiger's character dies after being hit with seven bullets, and Mr. Steiger made a big production of the scene, even saying a prayer to Heaven after being mortally wounded. After Mr. Steiger's character died, Terry-Thomas walked over and said, "I say, old boy, are you all right?"[19]

• Who says Marilyn Monroe didn't know how to act? When she made *The Prince and the Showgirl* with Laurence Olivier, the two stars grew to detest each other. In one scene, Ms. Monroe's character was supposed to flirt with Mr. Olivier's character. Ms. Monroe's Method acting coach, Paula Strasberg, told her, "Think of Frank Sinatra and Coca-Cola." The advice worked, and the scene worked.[20]

• Ben Affleck got to act with his favorite actor, Peter O'Toole, in the movie *Phantoms*. The location of the movie was in various very cold places in Colorado, and Mr. Affleck joked, "I would rather be in the Saudi Arabian desert." Mr. O'Toole, who had filmed *Lawrence of Arabia* in the Saudi Arabian desert, looked at Mr. Affleck and said quietly but firmly, "No, you wouldn't."[21]

• In 1939, Ralph Richardson played Captain Durrance in the film *The Four Feathers*. Captain Durrance is blinded by the African sun, and a scene in which he reads Braille contains an in-joke for fans of Mr. Richardson's performances in Shakespeare. The Captain uses Braille to read Caliban's speech, "The Isle is full of noises," then he says, "But of course I knew that speech by heart."[22]

• In 1962, Sydney Lumet directed Sir Ralph Richardson and Katherine Hepburn in the movie *Long Day's Journey into Night*. Once, Sir Ralph asked him a question about acting, and Mr. Lumet gave him an 11-minute answer. Sir Ralph looked at him — balefully, according to Mr. Lumet — then said, "Ah, I think I know what you want — a little more flute and a little less cello."[23]

• During the filming of Robert Altman's *Nashville*, he used a wide-screen Panavision frame. Actors were miked individually, and they didn't even know if they were in the frame in some of the crowd scenes. One of the actors asked Mr. Altman, "How will I know if I'm on camera?" He replied, "You won't. Just do something interesting, and you might end up in the picture."[24]

• One day, Orson Welles and Peter Bogdanovich were talking about movies — as usual — and they began to discuss the actress Greta Garbo, whom Mr. Welles adored. Mr. Bogdanovich lamented that she had made only two really good movies — *Camille* and *Ninotchka*. Mr. Welles was silent for a moment, and then he said, "You only need one." [25]

• Elizabeth Taylor and Richard Burton acted together in several movies, including *Cleopatra*. When Ms. Taylor proposed acting together in yet another movie, Mr. Burton declined, saying, "We don't want to become another Laurel and Hardy." Ms. Taylor replied, "Why? What's so bad about Laurel and Hardy?"[26]

• In 1983, Morgan Freeman auditioned for a small part in the movie *Harry and Son*, starring Paul Newman. Mr. Freeman did not get the role, but when Mr. Newman discovered that such a talented actor had not gotten a role in two years, he made sure that Mr. Freeman received another role in the movie.[27]

• While attending Yale University, movie actress Jodie Foster got a role in an off-campus student play — her first role on the stage. On opening night, she warned reporters that they had better write about more than just her — because if they wrote about just her, the other actors "will kill me."[28]

• Olsen and Johnson were a comedy team who made their best movies in the early 1940s. Harold Ogden (Chic) Johnson knew immediately that he wanted John Sigvard (Ole) Olsen as a partner because Ole was "the first man I ever heard imitate a busy signal on the telephone."[29]

• One of Marilyn Monroe's early roles consisted of walking across the stage in the Marx Brothers film *Love Happy*. When she met comedian Groucho Marx, he asked, "Can you walk?" She replied, "I learned to walk when I was a baby, and I haven't had a lesson since."[30]

• Lucille Ball was very happy when she learned that a part was available for a "Lucille Ball type." She let the movie studio know that she would be available in a week, but the studio decided that she wasn't the type they needed for the role.[31]

• Bert Lahr played the Cowardly Lion in *The Wizard of Oz*, but after that he didn't work much in films. He once explained why: "After *The Wizard of Oz* I was typecast as a lion, and there aren't all that many parts for lions."[32]

• In her old age, Katherine Hepburn suffered from a tremor in her voice and her face. Film critic Gene Siskel asked her why she continued to act with such a tremor. She replied, "What choice do I have?"[33]

Ad-libs

• Texas actor Marco Perella appeared in the TV movie *Fatal Deception: Mrs. Lee Harvey Oswald*. He played a Texas Lothario, while English Shakespearean actress Helena Bonham-Carter played Mrs. Oswald, who was a Russian immigrant with (of course) a Russian accent. Ms. Bonham-Carter is very small and very light, and Mr. Perella ad-libbed during a scene with her. He picked her up and danced with her, then raised her in his arms and dipped and twirled her and even put a piece of celery in his mouth and tickled her neck with it. All this time, Ms. Bonham-Carter was shrieking and giggling and whooping, and Mr. Perella was congratulating himself on doing something to make a renowned Shakespearean actress lose control — when suddenly he noticed that all the shrieks and all the giggles and all the whoops were being delivered by Ms. Bonham-Carter with an impeccable Russian accent. After the scene was shot, Ms. Bonham-Carter told him (with, of course, an impeccable English accent), "I say, dearie, that bit with the celery was perfectly ripping."[34]

• Both Mike Nichols and Elaine May could be hostile, and both were masters of the put-down. Ms. May, a beautiful woman, was once followed by two men who blew kisses at her. Never one to take BS, she turned around to face the men and asked them, "What's the matter? Tired of each other?" When one man replied, "F**k you," she replied, "With what?" While Mr. Nichols was directing *The Odd Couple*, he gave actor Walter Matthau a direction that the actor thought was emasculating, so he asked Mr. Nichols, "Mike, can I have my c**k back now?" Mr. Nichols yelled, "Props!"[35]

Advertising

• Bill Thomas was given the job of publicizing *It Ain't No Sin*, starring Mae West. He bought 100 parrots, trained them to say, "It ain't no sin," and was getting ready to send the parrots to newspaper editors and to the owners of movie theaters when he received upsetting news — the title of the movie had been changed.[36]

• Monty Python member John Cleese once asked a publicist, "What is the hardest kind of movie to publicize?" The publicist replied, "Anything original."[37]

Agents

• Quentin Tarantino wanted actor James Woods to star in his first movie, the hit *Reservoir Dogs*, so he made several cash offers to Mr. Woods' agent. Unfortunately, the agent never told Mr. Woods about the offers. Later, after Mr. Tarantino was famous, he met Mr. Woods and mentioned the offers to him. Mr. Woods was first surprised, then angry. He fired his agent.[38]

• Actor Montgomery Cliff wanted to make an important cameo in Stanley Kramer's 1961 movie *Judgment at Nuremberg*, but his agent nearly botched things by asking a very high fee for Mr. Cliff's services. Therefore, Mr. Cliff did the cameo for free, then sent his agent the agent's commission — in an empty paper sack.[39]

AIDS

• Anthony Perkins, the actor who played Norman Bates in Alfred Hitchcock's *Psycho*, died of AIDS in 1992. After he discovered that he was HIV-positive, he and his wife started to volunteer for Project Angel Food. This Los Angeles organization delivers food to men, women, and children who have AIDS. Mr. Perkins said, "There are many who believe that this disease is God's vengeance, but I believe it was sent to teach people how to love and understand and have compassion for each other."[40]

• Geoffrey Bowers worked as an attorney for a New York law firm, but when he contracted AIDS, the law firm fired him. He sued on the basis of discrimination, although he was worried that the lawsuit would upset his mother. However, his brother told him that "she didn't raise any of us to sit in the back of the bus." Later, the movie *Philadelphia*, starring Tom Hanks, was based in part on Mr. Bowers' experience.[41]

Airplanes

• Cliff Robertson once played an airplane pilot in a movie that required him to run through an airport. After Mr. Robertson had run five times through some corridors in the Los Angeles International Airport, the director called for a break. Being hot, tired, and thirsty, Mr. Robertson went into a bar at the airport, where he ordered a martini. After a few minutes, however, an official with the airline whose uniform Mr. Robertson was wearing asked him if he would please leave because he was upsetting the other customers — who thought he was a real pilot.[42]

• Howard Hughes was interested in Ingrid Bergman. After learning that she would be flying to Los Angeles on a certain date, Mr. Hughes immediately bought all the tickets to Los Angeles for that day, making it impossible for her to get a ticket, then he offered to fly her there in his private plane. He even arranged the flight schedule so he could give her an aerial tour of the Grand Canyon at dawn. Nevertheless, Ms. Bergman remained romantically uninterested in him.[43]

Alcohol

• Cartoonists Tex Avery and Michael Maltese once played a practical joke on an unsuspecting colleague by spiking a bottle of Coke in a vending machine. They removed the bottle cap, siphoned out some of the Coke, replaced it with a double shot of bourbon, and then put the bottle cap back on. The man who got the spiked Coke was a teetotaler, so he didn't recognize the taste of bourbon and he didn't enjoy drinking it. Instead, he spit it out and exclaimed, "I've been poisoned!"[44]

• W.C. Fields enjoyed playing havoc with the directors of his movies. On the set of *The Big Broadcast of 1938*, he performed a drinking scene that he had done the day before. When the director protested, Mr. Fields replied that the two scenes were different: "Yesterday, I did the scene with a bottle of gin. Today, I am doing it with a bottle of scotch."[45]

• In 1958, comedian Ernie Kovacs bought and remodeled a house in Hollywood. As a finishing touch for his wine cellar, he had the Columbia Pictures prop department come in and put cobwebs on all the wine bottles.[46]

• Film actor Humphrey Bogart stayed true to his tough-guy image. Just before he died, he said, "I should never have switched from Scotch to Martinis."[47]

Chapter 2: From Animals to Critics

Animals

• Billy Wilder once wanted to do a movie about the life of Vaslav Nijinsky, the gifted Russian dancer who ended up in an asylum, thinking he was a horse. Mr. Wilder explained his idea to studio head Samuel Goldwyn, who said, "Have you gone crazy? You want to make a picture about a man who thinks he's a horse?" Mr. Wilder knew then that the movie would not be made, so he replied, "We could always have a happy ending — we could show him winning the Derby."[48]

• Although actor Vincent Price liked most animals, he disliked horses, but unfortunately he occasionally had to ride them during the filming of his movies. John Stahl directed Mr. Price in *Forever Amber*, in which Mr. Price rode often. During the filming, Mr. Stahl used to shout at Mr. Price over the loudspeaker, "For God's sake, don't look so stupid on that horse, Vincent. Look as though you liked it." Mr. Price always replied, "But I don't like it, Mr. Stahl!"[49]

• Years after Jimmy Stewart made the movie *Harvey*, co-starring a six-foot-plus white rabbit that is invisible to most people, adults would ask him on the street — quite seriously — "Is Harvey with you?" Mr. Stewart's usual answer was, "No, Harvey has a cold, and he decided to stay home." To which grown men would reply, "Next time you see him, give him my regards, please."[50]

• French comedian Jacques Tati used some dogs that he picked up at the dog pound in *Mon Oncle*, an M. Hulot movie. After filming was over, he needed to find good homes for the dogs, so he advertised that they were movie stars. Every dog found a good home.[51]

• Charles Addams is known for his macabre cartoons that formed the premise of the TV series *The Addams Family*. After watching the premiere of *Cleopatra*, he was asked what he thought about the movie. He replied, "I only came to see the asp."[52]

• Many movies that are set in Spain or Italy are actually filmed in California. Bird-watchers sometimes get a kick out of watching one of these films and hearing the distinctive cries of California quail in the background.[53]

Audiences

• During World War II, British soldiers watched bad movies when that was the best entertainment available and often the only entertainment featuring female flesh. During one movie, the bad guy shot the good guy in the arm, and the well-endowed heroine tore off a strip of cloth from her blouse to use as a bandage. One British soldier yelled at the movie's bad guy, "Go on, shoot 'im in the other arm!"[54]

• When Charlie Chaplin's *Limelight* premiered in London, it was a great success. Mr. Chaplin was present, and after the film was over, he walked out on the stage and said "thank you" to the audience. However, a woman in the audience said, "No! No! Thank you!" Soon all the members of the audience were thanking Mr. Chaplin.[55]

• Mario Van Peebles' *New Jack City* contains a scene in which a character accepts drugs. When this scene was shown at a theater in New York City, an African-American man stood up and yelled at the screen, "Just say no, man!" Mr. Van Peebles says this is one of the best things he has witnessed in his life.[56]

Autographs

• Groucho Marx once sat for a caricature for the Brown Derby, a famous Hollywood restaurant on Vine Street. When the caricature was finished, he autographed it, "To Al Levy's Tavern — the best restaurant on Vine Street! Groucho Marx." Al Levy's Tavern was part of the competition, so the manager of the Brown Derby tore up the caricature. Years later, Groucho was asked to sit for another caricature for the Brown Derby, and he agreed — provided that the manager wouldn't censor his autograph. This time he wrote: "To the Hollywood Brown Derby — the best restaurant on Vine Street, but only because Al Levy's has gone out of business."[57]

• Opera singer Luciano Pavarotti comes from Modena, Italy, where people make sure not to give celebrities special treatment. Paul Newman visited Modena twice, where he ate in public restaurants twice. Both times, no one asked him for his autograph. He marveled, "What a polite city — no one bothered me." However, he couldn't help but wonder, "To interest the people of Modena, who do you have to be?"[58]

• A young boy once asked comedian W.C. Fields for his autograph. Mr. Fields glared at the boy, then said, "Go back to the reform school, you little nosepicker."[59]

Automobiles

• Wilson Mizner was an expert at deflating the pretentious. Once, he went to a Hollywood movie premiere where the fans were admiring the fabulously expensive limousines of the stars arriving at the theater. Mr. Mizner, however, arrived in a beat-up Ford. The driver of the car handed the keys to a haughty parking attendant who sneered at the car and then asked Mr. Mizner, "What shall I do with it?" Mr. Mizner said, "Keep it," and walked into the premiere.[60]

• Very early in his career, Lou Costello went to Hollywood in an unsuccessful attempt to break into the movies. He was so impoverished that he couldn't afford blankets, so on cold nights, he slept between mattresses. Later, he couldn't afford to rent a room, so he used to sleep in any unlocked car he found at night.[61]

Awards

• Hollywood actor Jimmy Stewart was made a Brigadier General in the Air Force Reserve, something that angered Senator Margaret Chase Smith, who believed that Mr. Stewart was unqualified. Discussing the promotion with such people as the Secretary of the Air Force and the Air Force Chief of Staff, she asked why he should be made Brigadier General and was told he deserved it because of his performance in the movie *Strategic Air Command*. Senator Smith was aghast and said, "Then why you don't make June Allyson a Brigadier General for playing the female lead in *Strategic Air Command*?" (Mr. Stewart turned out to be an exceptionally skilled and decorated military pilot who led 20 dangerous combat missions as a B-24 bomber pilot over Europe).[62]

• When Felicity Huffman won the Best Actress award at the Independent Spirit Awards for her performance as a transsexual in the movie *Transamerica*, she recounted a story about a grip working to correct some malfunctioning equipment. Perched precariously on a ladder, he muttered, "This f**king film better win a f**king award." Ms. Huffman then held her award up and said, "Here's the f**king award." [63]

Bathrooms

• Basil Rathbone and Nigel Bruce and their families once ate breakfast together while traveling on a train. Mr. Rathbone excused himself from the table, picked up the morning paper, then began to leave the dining car. Ever-mischievous Mr. Bruce asked Cynthia, Mr. Rathbone's young daughter, "Darling, where's Daddy going?" Cynthia's answer filled the crowded dining car: "Daddy's going to do after-breakfast plop-plops."[64]

• People frequently act strangely around celebrities. Humor writer H. Allen Smith tells a story about seeing Gary Cooper walk out of a men's room. Mr. Smith then entered the restroom, where a man standing at a urinal looked at him, grinned, and said, "Right on top of Gary Cooper's!"[65]

Birthdays

• Victoria Horne Oakie, the wife of comedian Jack Oakie (who played the Mussolini character in Charlie Chaplin's *Great Dictator*), had a wonderful idea for her husband's 70th birthday. For the year leading up to the birthday, she contacted hundreds of people her husband had worked with during his long career and asked them to write a letter to Jack. So many letters poured in that she had to collect them in two volumes. It took Mr. Oakie two weeks to read all the letters after dinner.[66]

• W.C. Fields used to lie about his birthday, giving several dates in various interviews. When asked why he did this, he replied that he wanted to get free drinks on those other days, too.[67]

Books

• Children's book author/illustrator Tomie dePaola eagerly looked forward to seeing the Walt Disney movie *Snow White and the Seven Dwarfs* when it came out in 1938, but he was surprised that the movie didn't follow the true version — that is, the version he knew — of the fairy tale. In the movie, the Evil Queen gave Snow White the poisoned apple without first pulling Snow White's laces so tight that she couldn't breathe or giving her a poisoned comb — both times, the dwarfs rescued her. This was so upsetting to Tomie that he yelled at the movie screen, "Where are the laces? Where is the comb?" In addition, he was so upset at the end of the movie — it stopped before the true ending — that he yelled at the screen again, "The story's not over yet. Where's the wedding? Where're the red-hot iron shoes that they put on the Evil Queen so that she dances herself to death?" His mother ran in from the lobby, where she had taken his younger brother when he became frightened during a scary scene, and dragged him out of the theater. Tomie saw the movie again with a little girl from the neighborhood, but he warned her in advance that Mr. Disney didn't know the true story of Snow White.[68]

• Believe it or not, producer Val Lewton's film *I Walked with a Zombie* is based in part on Charlotte Bronte's classic novel *Jane Eyre* — in the novel, Jane works for a man whose wife suffers from incurable insanity. Mr. Lewton's film studio, RKO, gave him a small budget and worried that his film was too arty, relying more on atmosphere than on blood to frighten people. One of his bosses complained about *I Walked with a Zombie* that "sock-it-to-them was being sacrificed for 'arty stuff.'" [69]

Censorship

• French comedian Jacques Tati, the creative genius behind the M. Hulot films, detested censorship, especially of his own work. Mr. Tati's film *Traffic* was to be shown in a movie theater at Champs-Elysées, but the management thought the film was too long, so they deleted a four-minute scene from it. However, when the film was shown, it included that scene because Mr. Tati had persuaded the projectionist to put the scene back in the film. Management again deleted the four-minute scene, but a few days later, the scene was back in the film because Mr. Tati had again persuaded the projectionist to put it back in the film.[70]

• Will Hays, the man in charge of censoring movies during the days when such things were done, was once upset because actress Lana Turner had shown too much cleavage in a movie, and so he scheduled a meeting with movie mogul Louis B. Mayer, who was prepared to argue that he ran a morally upright movie studio. Unfortunately for both men, comedian Harpo Marx found out about the meeting, and Harpo hired a stripper to peel to the bare essentials, then he chased her through the room where Mr. Hays and Mr. Mayer were meeting.[71]

• Alfred Hitchcock ran into a problem with the censors because of the shower scene in *Psycho*. The censors insisted that the scene showed nudity and the knife touching flesh. Mr. Hitchcock knew that the scene contained nothing of the kind but was edited to make the viewers think that that was what they were seeing. However, he agreed to make changes to the scene, waited a while, and then resubmitted the movie exactly as it had been when the censors saw it. This time, the censors agreed that the movie was OK.[72]

• Monty Python's satiric film *Life of Brian* treated Jesus Christ with great respect, but it aimed deadly barbs at organized religion. For this reason, it was banned by many theaters. For example, it was banned in Swansea, Wales. Fortunately, a financially struggling theater in Porthcawl, which is near Swansea, showed the movie, so Python fans traveled there to see *Life of Brian*. The film helped keep the movie theater from being forced to declare bankruptcy.[73]

• An interview with Mae West was once cancelled — that is, censored — by CBS-TV because of her comments. When *Person to Person* interviewer Charles Collingwood asked her about all the mirrors in her bedroom, she answered, "They're for personal observation. I always like to know how I'm doing." And when Mr. Collingwood attempted to change the subject to foreign affairs, Ms. West said, "I've always had a weakness for foreign affairs."[74]

• Early in his film career, Vincent Price thought that he had gotten his big break in a film in which he portrayed King Charles. In his big scene in the movie, King Charles and Nell Gwyn played with some puppies on a large bed. Unfortunately, the young actress playing Nell Gwyn was wearing such a low-cut dress and had such large breasts that the censors cut the scene out of the movie.[75]

• The Marx Brothers are known for their comedic rejection of authority and embrace of anarchy, which is probably why Benito Mussolini hated them. Mussolini ordered his subjects in the fall of 1939 not to laugh at the Marx Brothers.[76]

• Movie director John Waters knows how to keep censors happy — get a can of creamed corn and film a vomit scene so that the censors can cut it from the film.[77]

Charity

• Comedian Richard Pryor's private life was sometimes erratic. Once, he was charged with assault with a deadly weapon. He was fined $500, ordered to get rid of his gun collection, and given the choice to do 10 benefit performances or go to jail for four months. His attorney, Jack Tanner, asked the judge if a $100,000 donation that Mr. Pryor had given to the Jerry Lewis Muscular Dystrophy Telethon would be acceptable in lieu of the 10 benefit performances. Mr. Pryor, however, was unwilling for his donation to be used in that way. He said, "That was for charity. I didn't do it on account of this case, and I don't want it to count as part of my sentence."[78]

• The great dancer Bill Robinson, aka Mr. Bojangles, was known for his charity as well as his appearances in movies with Shirley Temple. During the Depression, the 132nd Precinct Station in Harlem kept a list of people it could turn to when a good deed was needed — such as buying a family a bag of groceries or paying for a funeral or paying the doctor bill of an ill child. Mr. Bojangles' name was at the top of the list. [79]

Children

• Many people are familiar with the Oscar-winning 1950 classic film comedy *Harvey* starring Jimmy Stewart as Elwood P. Dowd, a tippler who is befriended by a pooka named Harvey. (A pooka is a Celtic fairy spirit that frequently appears as an animal — always very large. In this particular case, Harvey is a six-foot-plus white rabbit.) Unfortunately, to most people pookas are invisible — Harvey chooses very carefully the people by whom he is seen. Such people are usually harmless rumpots or crackpots. Before *Harvey* became a movie, it was a play. Once, several children attended a theater performance featuring Mr. Stewart and his invisible friend. During Act I, all went well. But during Act II, Mr. Stewart noticed more and more children whispering to their parents. Finally, one child couldn't stand it any longer. He stood up and yelled, "WHERE'S THE RABBIT?"[80]

• Marilyn Harris played the little girl whom Frankenstein's Monster drowned in the movie *Frankenstein*, starring Boris Karloff. In the brief scene, part of which was later edited out, the Monster throws the little girl into the lake, thinking that she will float like a flower. Two takes were needed for the scene, but little Marilyn didn't want to be thrown into the lake a second time. Therefore, the director, James Whale, promised to give her anything she wanted if she did the scene a second time. She agreed, and she asked for a dozen hard-boiled eggs. A week later, Mr. Whale sent her two dozen hard-boiled eggs.[81]

• The great dancer Bill Robinson, aka Mr. Bojangles, was very protective of Shirley Temple, the child actress with whom he starred in several films. While working in films together, they were known as "One-Shot Temple and Robinson" because they made so few mistakes. One day, Shirley made a mistake, and Mr. Robinson said, "Why don't you let that child alone? She's hungry and she's tired." He then insisted on a 15-minute break, during which he ate some ice cream. Shirley was chubby then and not allowed to eat ice cream, but he gave her some ice cream when no one was looking.[82]

• Musical comedy star Donald O'Connor of *Singin' in the Rain* fame was on stage when he was three days old. His mother was in a vaudeville troupe, and she played piano as she recovered from the pregnancy. As she played, baby Donald was on the piano bench beside her. At 13 months, he was dancing on stage. Well, he wasn't actually dancing — one of his parents held him up and he moved his feet as fast as he could.[83]

• In San Francisco, comedian Robin Williams (among other roles he has played, his voice is the voice of the genie in the Disney movie *Aladdin*) stopped in at a Disney store. A mother shopping there recognized him and told her young son, "Look, honey. It's the genie from *Aladdin*." The child looked at Mr. Williams, but seemed confused. Then the child smiled — behind Mr. Williams was a big picture of the *Aladdin* genie.[84]

• Will Rogers became famous first for his tricks with a rope, then for his jokes as a comedian, and finally for his skills as an actor. However, he didn't want his own children to be actors. One day, he was very annoyed by a stage mother who was trying to get her child a role in one of his movies. After finally getting rid of her, Mr. Rogers told his own children, "I'm glad you don't have any talent."[85]

• Even as a two-year-old child, Wah Ming Chang enjoyed drawing. He especially liked to draw lambs, and he enjoyed putting the pictures he drew under his mother's pillow as a surprise gift for her. Later, he became a famous artist and an Oscar-winning creator of special effects for the movies *Tom Thumb* and *The Time Machine*.[86]

• When the mother of children's book author/illustrator Tomie dePaola was a little girl, she and her father went every week for 14 weeks to a movie theater to watch a serial adventure movie. Unfortunately, before they were able to watch the end of the serial, the movie theater was torn down, so they never did learn how it ended.[87]

• Pistol Pete Maravich was a high scorer throughout his career. As a kid, he was always found with a basketball. He even used to dribble while riding his bike, and when he went to the movies, he carried a basketball with him so he could watch the movie while dribbling the basketball in the aisle.[88]

• A young man who said he was W.C. Fields' son came to visit the famous comedian. Mr. Fields asked the young man what he wanted to drink and after the young man asked for a Coke, Mr. Fields yelled for his butler and ordered him to throw the young man out because "he's no son of mine."[89]

Clothing

• While attending Morehouse College, Spike Lee directed the coronation pageant, one of the biggest events of homecoming. Students dressed up nicely for the pageant, and the women usually wore slinky, revealing dresses. However, as director of the pageant, Mr. Lee decided to emulate old Hollywood musicals, and he wanted the women to be dressed in floor-length, not-so-revealing evening gowns. The male students wanted to see the women in revealing dresses, so when they learned about his plans, they threatened him, but the pageant came off as Mr. Lee had planned.[90]

• Katherine Hepburn's movie studio wanted her to dress stylishly all the time, but when she wasn't acting, Ms. Hepburn preferred to wear comfortable clothing such as jeans. Therefore, the movie studio stole her jeans one day as she was acting. Ms. Hepburn sent the movie studio VIPs word that if her jeans were not returned, she would walk around naked. She didn't walk around naked, but she did walk around wearing silk panties. The movie studio returned her jeans.[91]

• A smart person with power is actress Julia Roberts, star of *Pretty Woman*. In the 1991 movie *Sleeping with the Enemy*, she had to film a scene wearing only panties and an undershirt, so she ordered the entire production crew to strip down to their underwear, too. She said later, "We all had a laugh and the night went a lot faster — because anybody working in his underwear wants to get done a little quicker!"[92]

• When Marlene Dietrich was a big star in Hollywood, she frequently wore gender-bending clothing such as men's tuxedos. In fact, at one time she was called "The Best Dressed Man in Hollywood," and some newspapers referred to her and her clothing as "Mr. Dietrich and his fabulous wardrobe."[93]

• Olympic gold-medalist figure skater Sonja Henie felt very comfortable wearing her ice skates. In fact, when she felt uncomfortable filming a romantic scene with Tyrone Power for a movie, she mentioned that she would feel a lot more comfortable in the scene if she could wear her ice skates.[94]

Crime

• Filmmaker John Waters once worked as a teacher in a prison. Once a year, a graduation ceremony was held in the prison for all student-convicts who were receiving a college degree. After the ceremony, convicts and their families were allowed to attend a barbeque, and Mr. Waters remembers one of the graduates telling his father that he was doing well and hoped to be paroled soon, and that when he was paroled he would renovate the family home. Just then, his father asked, referring to the plate his son the convict was holding, "Are you through with that?" His son wasn't sure what he was referring to and replied, "With what? Killing people or eating?"[95]

• Controversial filmmaker John Waters was once mugged in New York. Suffering from a serious concession and covered with blood, he staggered to a friend's apartment, and when she opened the door, he told her, "I've just killed five people, and I've come to involve you."[96]

Critics

• Film critic Jim Emerson met famed director Robert Altman by accident in a hotel. Mr. Emerson had recently returned from Europe, and he was telling a publicist how he "found it exhilarating and liberating to be in a strange city, and to be out in public, and not understand the conversations that are taking place all around you." Mr. Altman was nearby, talking on a telephone, and when his telephone conversation was over, he came up to Mr. Emerson and said, "I heard what you were saying about being in Europe, and that's exactly the way I've felt! I lived in Paris for years and never learned French. You realize there's just so much extraneous bullsh*t you don't have to listen to if you don't know the language!"[97]

• John Simon was introduced to Laura Mulvey at the 1977 Berlin Film Festival. During the introduction, he learned that Ms. Mulvey had recently completed a film with Peter Wollen. Mr. Simon, a caustic critic, said to her, "How could you work with that man Peter Wollen, that no-talent, phony semiologist!" Later that day, one of Mr. Simon's friends told him, "You do realize that Laura Mulvey is married to Peter Wollen, don't you? She wanted to know whether you were always so disgustingly rude to everybody."[98]

• When Diana Rigg was compiling her book of the worst-ever theatrical reviews, *No Turn Unstoned*, she wrote to several actors and actresses, asking them for the worst-ever theatrical review they had ever received. Miss Piggy, who was Ms. Rigg's co-star in *The Great Muppet Caper*, sent her this "worst-ever" review: "She may be the screen's sexiest star since Marilyn Monroe."[99]

• Quentin Crisp once attended a screening of *King Kong* with a friend. During a scene in which Fay Wray's character lay screaming in King Kong's palm, the friend said to Mr. Crisp, "I can't think what he sees in her."[100]

Chapter 3: From Dance to Husbands and Wives

Dance

• Fred Astaire wore a hairpiece — which he hated — throughout his career. In 1946, he thought that he would retire after filming a movie titled *Blue Skies*. After filming the final scene of the movie, Mr. Astaire took off his hairpiece, threw it on the floor, and started jumping on it, shouting, "Never, never, never — never will I have to wear this blasted rug again!"[101]

• W.C. Fields felt respect for and threatened by the comedy genius of rival comedian Charles Chaplin. He once sat silently during a Chaplin movie that had other members of the audience roaring with laughter. Asked after the movie was over for his opinion of Mr. Chaplin, Mr. Fields said, "He's a ballet dancer, the best ballet dancer that ever lived, and if I get a good chance, I'll kill him with my bare hands."[102]

• Fred Astaire was once staying at the home of Jock Whitney, and he asked Mr. Whitney to teach him a new dance called the Sluefoot. Big mistake. Mr. Whitney wasn't able to get any sleep that night. Mr. Astaire stayed up all night practicing the Sluefoot, and his bedroom was located directly above Mr. Whitney's.[103]

Death

• In a movie stunt, actor Sheldon Leonard was supposed to be under a truck that was held up by a hoist. The truck was to be lowered toward him, then stopped by pushing a button just before it crushed him. Before doing the stunt, Mr. Leonard said, "Let me see how it works." The director didn't want to demonstrate, arguing that it had taken two hours to light the scene and he didn't want to move the truck, but Mr. Leonard insisted. As the truck was lowered, the filmmaker pushed the stop button, but the truck kept descending onto the spot where Mr. Leonard's corpse would have been if he hadn't insisted on seeing a demonstration of the stop button. The hoist's stop button had worked perfectly for light passenger cars, but the truck was too heavy for the hoist.[104]

• In his movie *Roger and Me*, director Michael Moore included footage of a white woman slaughtering a rabbit by clubbing it to death. Many people have told Mr. Moore how upset they were by the scene. However, two minutes later in the movie appears footage in which Flint, Michigan, police shoot and kill a black man who is holding a toy gun and wearing a Superman costume. In his book *Stupid White Men*, Mr. Moore writes, "Not once — not *ever* — has anyone said to me, 'I can't believe you showed a black man being shot in your movie! How horrible! How disgusting! I couldn't sleep for weeks.'"[105]

• Charlie Chaplin died on Christmas of 1977, and on December 27, he was laid to rest in a cemetery in Vevey, Switzerland. However, on March 2, 1978, his coffin was dug up by grave robbers and carried away with his body inside it. The grave robbers demanded 600,000 francs for the return of the body. Fortunately, the police were able to capture the grave robbers as they attempted to pick up the ransom. Mr. Chaplin's body was recovered, and the grave robbers were put on trial and convicted.[106]

• Mischa Auer provided comic support in many films of the 1930s and 1940s, including the classics *My Man Godfrey*, *You Can't Take It With You*, and *Destry Rides Again*. Mr. Auer had a hard early life in St. Petersburg, Russia, losing both parents — his mother died of typhus, and his father died in the Russo-Japanese War. After immigrating to the United States, he found it difficult to concentrate on his education, and he once told a teacher, "After seeing death and torture, suppose I don't do algebra."[107]

• Sometimes fans act like jerks. In John Barrymore's funeral procession, his friends, many of whom were famous stars, drove by a sidewalk crowded with fans who cheered as the stars went by. W.C.

Fields, mourning the death of one of his best friends, looked at the crowd of fans and said, "God-d*mn morons!"[108]

• Death is not optional. After Samuel Goldwyn had criticized her for writing her movie scripts too sad and without happy endings, Dorothy Parker replied, "Mr. Goldwyn, since the world was created, billions and billions of people have lived, and not a single one has had a happy ending."[109]

• British actress Hermione Gingold once was asked if her most recent of several husbands was dead. She replied, "That's a matter of opinion."[110]

Education

• Often, geniuses are not satisfied even with works of genius. Frank Capra once visited a film class taught by Professor Jeanine Basinger of Wesleyan College. In the class she showed *Mr. Smith Goes to Washington*, which of course starred Jimmy Stewart and which Mr. Capra had directed. He strolled the college grounds for most of the film but returned in time to see the end, including the scene in which Mr. Stewart's character breaks down. Although this scene (and the entire film) is a classic, Mr. Capra became upset. Ms. Basinger asked him what was wrong, and Mr. Capra explained, "I shouldn't have done it that way. It could have been better."[111]

• Will Rogers was once asked to be toastmaster at a Jewish charitable club and he surprised everybody, including comedian Eddie Cantor, by speaking Yiddish. According to Mr. Cantor, "It seems the minute he was asked to be toastmaster, he got hold of a young student who in six weeks taught him enough of the language so that he could conduct the program."[112]

• Phyllis Diller's first movie starred Bob Hope: *Boy, Did I Get a Wrong Number!* On the set, Mr. Hope noticed Ms. Diller looking around. After asking, he found out that she was looking for the cue cards. "Phyllis, we don't use cue cards in movies," Mr. Hope explained.

"That's only in television." Ms. Diller was surprised: "Oh? Then I'd better learn my lines."[113]

Fans

• Professional golfer Peter Jacobsen has seen actor Samuel L. Jackson at many celebrity golf tournaments, and he knows that Mr. Jackson often goes across the rope separating the golfers from the crowd of fans so he can mingle with the fans. Of course, many celebrities are leery of doing that — sometimes with good reason — so Mr. Jacobsen asked Mr. Jackson why he did that. Mr. Jackson explained, "Because, Peter, these are the people who allow me to be playing here. They go see my movies, they buy the DVDs, they make me who I am. And I greatly appreciate their support of me and my work." Mr. Jacobsen observes with admiration, "How impressive is that?"[114]

• While actor Paul Newman was in Kansas City to film *Mr. and Mrs. Bridge*, he went into an ice cream shop, where he met one of the local citizens, who was flustered to see a big movie star. The woman paid for her ice cream, then left the ice cream shop. A few moments later, she realized that she didn't have her ice cream in her hand, so she returned to the shop. Mr. Newman asked her, "Are you looking for your ice cream?" Still flustered, the woman could only nod. Mr. Newman then told her, "You put it in your purse with your change."[115]

• Beautiful actress/model June Wilkinson made a movie in Mexico titled *The Rage Within*. Her male co-star was in love with her, and his house was filled with her photographs. The night before they were to film a big scene, they went on a date, and he tried to kiss her. However, Ms. Wilkinson declined to be kissed, and the leading man grew angry and told her, "Your pictures are sexier than you are!" The next day, the director asked her, "Are you ready for your big love scene? How was your date?" She replied, "I think we're in trouble."[116]

• Andy Robinson played a psycho killer in *Dirty Harry*. No, he did not play Dirty Harry — he played the other psycho killer. This movie has a famous scene at the end in which Dirty Harry holds a gun that may or may not contain a bullet on Mr. Robinson's character and asks him, "Do you feel lucky? Well, do you, punk?" In real life Mr. Robinson is a committed pacifist, and unfortunately in real life strangers sometimes recognize him and say to him, "Do you feel lucky? Well, do you, punk?"[117]

• When Baz Luhrmann's *William Shakespeare's Romeo + Juliet* first came out, Ohio University Shakespeare scholar Samuel Crowl saw it at his local cineplex, where he was surprised by the number of teenyboppers who had come to see Leonardo DiCaprio play Romeo. When Mr. DiCaprio's Romeo and Claire Danes' Juliet first met, a young DiCaprio fan sitting behind Professor Crowl whispered, "Don't touch him, you b*tch."[118]

• Gerard Depardieu once met a couple in a Parisian hotel, where the hotel manager was immensely impressed by such a famous guest. He came over to the table of three, asked Mr. Depardieu what he wanted to order to drink, received the order — a glass of red wine — then rushed off to fill the order, completely ignoring the other two people at the table.[119]

• Late in Peter Lorre's career, after he had begun to make bad films, a fan wrote him, "I would love to be tortured by you." Mr. Lorre wrote back, "You have been tortured enough by going to my pictures."[120]

Fathers

• Professional golfer Peter Jacobsen once played at a tournament with actor Clint Eastwood, and he brought his father along so he could be impressed. Unfortunately, his father did not recognize Mr. Eastwood — something that tickled one of the most famous actors (and directors) in the world. Mr. Eastwood mentioned a number of movies he had made, including the spaghetti westerns and the Dirty Harry movies, but Mr. Jacobsen's father had not seen those movies. Eventually, Mr. Eastwood mentioned that early in his career he had been in *Rawhide*, and Mr. Jacobsen's father said, "Oh, yeah. You were

Rowdy .... I loved that show." Mr. Jacobsen's father started calling Mr. Eastwood "Rowdy," and the two men got along very well indeed.[121]

• Jack Benny, a Jewish comedian, made a film titled *To Be or Not to Be*, in which he wore a Nazi uniform and said such dialogue as "Heil Hitler." Mr. Benny's father saw the beginning of the film, then walked out and refused to speak to his son on the telephone for a long time, saying that Jack was no longer his son. Finally, Mr. Benny was able to speak to his father and explain that he had been misled by the beginning of the film — if his father would see all of the film, he would know that the character was actually fighting against the Nazis, not for them. Mr. Benny's father returned to the movie theater and saw all of the film — a total of 46 times.[122]

• As a boy, Lou Costello and his brother once played hooky from school, so they could see a Western at the local movie theater. When the movie ended, they discovered that their father, who also loved Westerns, was sitting behind them. Later in life, Mr. Costello made Universal Pictures hire his father as consultant to *The Wistful Widow of Wagon Gap*, an Abbott and Costello comedy Western.[123]

Food

• When André Previn was working on the set of *Porgy and Bess*, he ran into a studio security officer who didn't recognize him. One day, Mr. Previn took a break and brought back tea and doughnuts for the other people working on the movie. The security officer told him that it was a closed set, but let him in after asking if the set was expecting a delivery of tea and doughnuts. After that, the only way Mr. Previn could get past this security officer was to bring in tea and doughnuts. One day, Mr. Previn was on the podium conducting the orchestra when the security officer came in, looked at him, and said, "Sonny, get the hell off the podium — the conductor's liable to be here any minute." [124]

• Throughout his movie career, Mario Lanza gained and (usually) lost weight very quickly. In some of his movies, he seems to gain and lose weight between scenes. Sometimes, a thin Mario will walk into a building, but inside the building a fat Mario is acting. For one movie, the movie studio had Mario's costumes made in three different sizes: normal, big, and obese. Of course, the movie studio tried to keep his weight under control, but he outfoxed them by doing such things as ordering from room service three different meals using three different names so he could eat as much as he wanted.[125]

• It's not a good idea to ignore the Marx Brothers. On one occasion, after producer Irving Thalberg had excused himself for a minute from a story conference with the Marx Brothers and then did not return, the Marx Brothers shoved file cabinets against Mr. Thalberg's door so that he couldn't enter his office. Another time, Mr. Thalberg left a meeting with the Marx Brothers in order to talk to someone else. When he returned, the Marx Brothers were sitting naked in his office, roasting potatoes in his fireplace. Mr. Thalberg laughed, then ordered butter to be brought to his office for the potatoes.[126]

• Food can be hard to come by early in a career, even when someone becomes a major success later. Working as a model in Chicago, Halle Berry shared a one-bedroom apartment with many roommates. Most of whatever money they had went to pay the rent, leaving little for food. The women made do by going to bars that served free appetizers such as barbequed chicken wings. And when Ms. Berry moved to New York City to become an actress, she spent some nights sleeping in a homeless shelter.[127]

• Comedian Joe E. Brown was born and grew up near Toledo, Ohio. While growing up, he was poor and sometimes hungry. His father was a honest house painter, which apparently was not a good thing to be in the winter. Mr. Brown remembers one winter when meat for the family's supper depended on his father coming home each day with a rabbit he had hunted. The family used to eat lard sandwiches — lard spread on bread and sprinkled with salt.[128]

• Movie stars Ben Affleck and Matt Damon lived very close to each other as they grew up in Boston. Matt's mother taught him how to cook — a fact that was not lost on other mothers. In fact, Ben's mother tried to convince him to help out more around the house by telling him that Matt cooked twice a week for his family. Ben jokes, "I first knew him as a guy who was setting a really bad precedent in the neighborhood."[129]

• Thelma Todd was an attractive platinum-blonde comedian who appeared in 1930s movies with ZaSu Pitts and the Marx Brothers. Her boss, Hal Roach, wanted her to stay attractive, so her contract included a clause stating that she had to keep her weight to within five pounds of what it was when she signed her contract — otherwise, she would be fired. This was known as the "potato clause."[130]

• Laurel and Hardy created the most massive pie fight in history in their movie short *Battle of the Century*. To make the short, they bought one day's production of the Los Angeles Pie Company — a total of 4,000 pies. The short used every pie. (Comedians need special skills. Silent film comedian Fatty Arbuckle was ambidextrous, and using either hand, he could hit a target 10 feet away with a pie.)[131]

• Movie star Mario Lanza insisted for one of his movies that the crew and extras be served the same meals that the stars were served instead of the simple meal of a slice of prosciutto and a hard roll that they had been eating. The movie studio charged Mr. Lanza for the extra cost. He said, "At least, I don't have to sit around choking on my food because everyone is watching me eat."[132]

• People in Russia and in the former USSR had it rough — even famous figure skaters had trouble getting food. Figure skater Alexander Zhulin remembers watching a movie about a prison, and he says that "all I could concentrate on was the prisoners were eating all this wonderful food."[133]

• When Allen Ludden and Betty White moved to California, actor Pat O'Brien, their new neighbor, wasted no time in introducing himself. Carrying a cup of sugar, he walked over to their house and said, "I thought I'd save you the trip next door to borrow this."[134]

• Famous insult comedian Groucho Marx once went to a restaurant, where he saw a woman seated by herself. He asked her, "Are you alone?" When she answered yes, Groucho told her, "Then there must be something terribly wrong with you."[135]

• George Lucas, the writer and director of *American Graffiti* and *Star Wars*, likes his privacy. He once was recognized in a restaurant — that was the last time he ate there.[136]

Friends

• Movie writer-director-actor Kevin Smith met Bryan Johnson when they were teenagers hanging out at the local community center. Bryan had just broken up with his high-school girlfriend, and Kevin asked him, "Can I have her?" This made Bryan laugh, and they became friends. Bryan plays obnoxious comic-book fan Steve-Dave in several of Kevin's movies, including *Mallrats* and *Jay and Silent Bob Strike Back*. [137]

• The young Audrey Hepburn was once asked to wear a padded bra for an advertisement. At first she didn't want to, but Frederic Mullally (her press agent) convinced her to do the ad. Mr. Mullally saved a copy of Ms. Hepburn's ad and inscribed it, "Audrey Hepburn — and friends."[138]

Gambling

• Chico Marx loved to gamble and so he never saved a dime of the hundreds of thousands of dollars he made and thus had to be supported in his old age by his thriftier brothers, Groucho and Harpo. One day, Salwyn Shufro (Groucho's financial advisor) asked Chico to guess how much money he had lost through gambling. Chico replied that he could tell exactly how much money he had gambled away, then asked how much money Groucho had in the bank. The reply came back: "Approximately $750,000." Chico smiled and then said, "That's how much money I've lost gambling."[139]

• Paul Newman played the role of pool shark "Fast Eddie" in the movie *The Hustler*. Ever since the movie came out, people have challenged him to compete in games of pool — for money. Often, someone says to him, "Hey, we don't have to play for much — what do you want to play for?" When that happens, Mr. Newman looks the person straight in the eyes and replies, "How about your house?" The would-be hustler then backs down, and Mr. Newman is able to keep his money in his own pocket instead of transferring it to the hustler's pocket.[140]

Gays and Lesbians

• Due to TV's *Buffy the Vampire Slayer*, the heterosexual Alyson Hannigan became a gay icon because she played Willow Rosenberg, a character who had a positive same-sex relationship with the character Tara Maclay, played by Amber Benson. However, in an alternate universe the gay icon may be Sarah Michelle Gellar, who played Buffy. In the movie *Cruel Intentions*, Sarah played a character who had some lesbian scenes, and in fact, her character's lesbian kiss with the character played by Selma Blair won an award for Best Screen Kiss at the MTV Movie Awards. Shortly afterward, Sarah filmed the movie *Scoobie-Doo*, in which her character, Daphne, exchanges bodies with the character Fred, then kisses the character played by Linda Cardellini. For a while, Sarah was excited that her second on-screen, same-sex kiss might win for her a second award for Best Screen Kiss at the MTV Movie Awards, but unfortunately, that scene ended up on the cutting-room floor, disappointing lesbians everywhere.[141]

• Michael Thomas Ford once attended a screening of *What Ever Happened to Baby Jane?* in a New York theater filled with gay men. As the movie was shown on the screen, half of the audience recited Bette Davis' lines from memory, while the other half recited Joan Crawford's lines from memory.[142]

Gifts

• One of Marlene Dietrich's heroes was Alexander Fleming, the discoverer of penicillin. As an entertainer of GIs in Europe during World War II, Ms. Dietrich knew that Mr. Fleming's discovery had saved the lives of thousands of soldiers. When she had the chance five years after the war, she invited him to dinner. After dinner, Mr. Fleming gave Ms. Dietrich a gift — a small glass jar containing the very first penicillin culture.[143]

• Canadian figure skater Toller Cranston once did a movie with Artur Rubinstein, after which Mr. Rubinstein gave him five gallons of a very expensive Guerlain men's cologne in a cut-glass decanter. It was impossible to use that much cologne in the regular way — so Mr. Cranston took a bath in it.[144]

Husbands and Wives

• Celebrities sometimes must have long-distance relationships with loved ones because of their work. When actress Halle Berry was making the TV movie *Solomon and Sheba* in Africa, she was separated from her then-husband, baseball player David Justice, by an ocean. For the first month they were apart, their long-distance telephone bill was $4,500. In October of 1995, Mr. Justice won the World Series for his team — the Braves — by hitting a home run. Ms. Berry was watching the game on TV — 3,000 miles away because she was making a movie. [145]

• Ballet dancer Jacques d'Amboise courted another dancer, Caroline George, but he got off to a bad start with her family. They were conservative, and so being a male ballet dancer was bad, in their opinion. In addition, he showed up with long hair (a no-no) that had been dyed red (another no-no) for his role in the movie *Seven Brides for Seven Brothers*. Finally, he tried to show off his knowledge of the wines of Europe, then discovered that her family didn't drink. Still, all ended well. He and Caroline (aka Carrie) married and had children.[146]

• Ilka Chase was once married briefly to the much-married actor Louis Calhern. After her divorce, she sent a box of calling cards engraved "Mrs. Louis Calhern" to Julia Hoyt, Mr. Calhern's next wife, with the note, "Dear Julia: I hope these reach you in time."[147]

• Actor Robert Morley's wife once tried to bluff her way into a hotel dining room that had been reserved for General Motors. She told the hotel staff, "The General is a good friend of mine. He will be delighted to see me." (The bluff didn't work.)[148]

• Actress Pia Zadora was very young when she married Meshulam "Rik" Riklis, a much older, very wealthy man. When she became pregnant, he was very happy and joked to her, "Now you'll have somebody your own age to play with."[149]

Chapter 4: From Insults to Prejudice

Insults

• Don't mispronounce the names of people who have sharp tongues. Hollywood actress Jean Harlow once approached the wife of the Prime Minister of England, and said, "Why, you must be Margot Asquith," mispronouncing her name by pronouncing the 't' in "Margot." Ms. Asquith replied, "No, my dear, the 't' is silent, as in 'Harlow.'"[150]

• Groucho Marx was known for his ability to insult people. This did have a disadvantage. Dick Cavett says that Groucho once complained that he couldn't insult anyone anymore. Some people he wanted to insult, but when he insulted them, they laughed, and then they told other people, "Did you hear what Groucho just said to me?" [151]

Language

• When Hispanic actor Antonio Banderas first came to the United States to make movies, he did not speak English, although he was good at making English speakers think that he spoke English. When he met Arne Glimcher, who was to direct him in *The Mambo Kings*, he kept slapping him on the back, grabbing his arm and laughing, and saying a few English words such as "oh, yeah," "of course," and "right, right." Eventually, Mr. Glimcher said to him, "You don't understand a word I'm saying, do you?" Mr. Banderas responded by smiling and laughing. That was when Mr. Glimcher knew that he was in the presence of the actor he wanted to star in his movie. (Mr. Banderas did learn English for real and very quickly — he studied it eight hours a day so he could speak English in *The Mambo Kings*.)[152]

• Actor Eli Wallach attempted to learn French by watching French films. During World War II, he had dinner with a free French family in Casablanca. After dinner, the family's child was sent off to bed, so Mr. Wallach said to the child a few words that he had learned from a movie.

To his horror, he learned that instead of saying "Kiss me good night," as he had intended, he had said, "Sleep with me."[153]

Makeup

• While making the B horror movie *Evil Dead* in rural Tennessee, actor Bruce Campbell was frequently covered in fake blood made in part from Karo Syrup. Sometimes, he would film all night, get in the back of a pickup truck while still covered in "blood," then pass spit-polished families going to church. He always smiled, waved, and pretended that everything was absolutely normal.[154]

• Comedian Robin Williams dressed in drag when the character he was playing in *Mrs. Doubtfire* disguised himself as an elderly nanny. The disguise was very effective. While filming in North Beach, California, Mr. Williams — dressed as Mrs. Doubtfire — stopped at a newsstand and looked through *Playboy*. A college student saw him and told a friend, "That old lady sure is hip, man."[155]

• Debbie Reynolds starred in many musicals as a dancer and singer. It's not always a glamorous job — dancers sweat a lot and sometimes have to yell for pits makeup. When that happens, the dancer raises her arms in the air, and the makeup person mops up the sweat and powders the dancer's armpits.[156]

Mishaps

• Jason Mewes is the comedic genius who plays the uninhibited foul-mouthed Jay to movie writer-director-actor Kevin Smith's Silent Bob in such movies as *Jay and Silent Bob Strike Back*. Jay and Silent Bob made a short but memorable appearance in the excellent film *Chasing Amy*. Since Mr. Mewes had not been acting for a while, Mr. Smith worried that he would not have his lines memorized, so Mr. Smith told his crew that they might be working for a while, perhaps filming Mr. Mewes performing one line of dialogue, then pausing as he memorized the next line so he could perform it, and so on. However, when it came time to record the scene, Mr. Mewes sailed through his dialogue with no problem whatsoever, and it was Mr. Smith who kept forgetting his lines. Afterwards, the crew teased Mr. Smith, saying, "Oh, yeah, Kevin, we better watch out for this Mewes character — we're gonna be here all night."[157]

• While filming a scene in the movie *Awakenings*, Robin Williams' character was required to restrain Robert De Niro's character. Mr. Williams heard a loud pop, knew that he had accidentally broken Mr. De Niro's nose, and started exclaiming, "Oh, no! Oh, God! Oh, Jesus!" Director Penny Marshall thought at first that he was overacting, but as soon as she saw the blood streaming down Mr. De Niro's face, she realized what had happened. Mr. De Niro insisted on filming the scene nine more times, because his doctor wasn't available yet, and he knew that his face was going to swell up and he wouldn't be able to film for a week. Of course, Mr. De Niro was annoyed by the accident, but his nose had previously been broken, and Mr. Williams broke his nose in such a way that it was pushed back to where it belonged. The accident actually improved Mr. De Niro's appearance.[158]

• Hollywood cameraman James "Jimmy" Wong Howe remembers a few bad times involving guns during his long career. Once, he was filming a prison from an airplane. He saw the prison guards pointing their rifles at him but figured that they were simply making the scene more realistic. Later, he learned that they had been shooting at the airplane because the permit allowing him to film the prison had not arrived on time. On another occasion, several Mexican extras were given blank guns to shoot in a battle scene. However, some of the extras didn't like each other, so they actually put small pellets in the guns — 50 people were hurt.[159]

• Mexico-born Nicholas Magallanes had a few mishaps in his ballet career. While taking a break during the filming of the ballet *A Midsummer Night's Dream*, he chewed on a breath mint. When filming resumed, he was instructed to open his mouth wide, which he did. However, the scene had to be filmed again — his tongue was bright green. On another occasion, this time involving live dance, he was engrossed in a game of chess in his dressing room. Having neglected to listen closely to the music during the performance, he was shocked to hear his entrance music coming over the PA system — he flew to the stage.[160]

• Laurel and Hardy's *Big Business* is a short film classic. In it, Laurel and Hardy are selling Christmas trees, and they get into an argument with James Finlayson — an argument that results in Laurel and Hardy deliberately destroying Mr. Finlayson's house. To make the film, producer Hal Roach rented the house of a vacationing family, paying them a large fee for the privilege of wrecking their house. Unfortunately, the film crew went to the wrong address — that of the house of a different vacationing family — so Laurel and Hardy wrecked the wrong house.[161]

• Phyllis Diller's first movie with Bob Hope was *Boy, Did I Get a Wrong Number!* In it, her character was supposed to ride a motorcycle, but her stunt double was unable to do this because she had broken her leg. Therefore, a short stunt man doubled for Ms. Diller, wearing her fright wig and funny clothing. Unfortunately for the male stunt double, Ms. Diller's husband visited the set, saw the male stunt double from behind, thought the male stunt double was Ms. Diller, and spun the male stunt double around and planted a big kiss on his lips.[162]

• Marlon Brando starred in the movie *Mutiny on the Bounty*, which was filmed on location in Tahiti. The director used several local women as extras in the movie, but because their natural endowments weren't up to Hollywood standards, he had them wear falsies. In one scene, the native women dove over the side of the ship, and their falsies came floating to the top of the water and they started playing catch with them. Unfortunately, this scene was cut from the motion picture.[163]

• In the Monty Python movie *Life of Brian*, Graham Chapman has a brief nude scene in which he appears before 300 Tunisian extras. The extras did not behave as expected, for the extras were Muslim, and their religion forbids women to see such scenes. So when Mr. Chapman suddenly opened some shutters and appeared naked before them, half of the extras — the women — ran away, screaming.[164]

• The weather in other countries can be difficult to figure out. While in Spain to make a motion picture, actor/director Robert Morley dismissed the film crew for the day because it was raining, then he went into a nearby bar. Ten minutes after he had dismissed the film crew, the sun was shining brightly and the sky was without a cloud.[165]

• Bruce Vilanch had a role as a fashion designer in the Diana Ross movie *Mahogany*, but he ruined the first take of his scene. He was supposed to be sewing in the scene, but he didn't know how to sew. He ended up sewing his scarf to Miss Ross' coat, and when Ms. Ross got up to leave, she started to drag him along with her.[166]

• While filming *Washington Square*, Sir Ralph Richardson astonished fellow actor Montgomery Cliff. Mr. Cliff flubbed take after take while Sir Ralph was perfect each time. Finally Mr. Cliff moaned about Sir Ralph, "Can't that man make any mistakes?"[167]

Money

• Will Rogers did not seem to take movie-making seriously. Usually, he declined to shoot a scene more than once. This meant that his movies were completed quickly and under schedule. However, this could have led to financial problems for his co-workers, who often had expected to work for longer than the movie actually took to complete. Will Rogers became very popular with his co-workers by using his own money to pay them their salaries for whatever extra time they would have worked if the movie had not been completed so quickly.[168]

• The major Marx Brothers were the witty Groucho, the fake-Italian Chico, and the silent Harpo. Also performing early in their comedy career was the straight-man Zeppo, who dropped out to become a very successful agent. After Zeppo dropped out of the act, movie producer Irving Thalberg inquired if perhaps the Marx Brothers would take a cut in salary because now they were only three Marx

Brothers instead of four Marx Brothers. Groucho replied, "Don't be silly. Without Zeppo, we're worth twice as much."[169]

• Goldwyn Studios used to have the policy that whenever it allowed one of its actors to appear on radio, it would receive half of that actor's fee. David Niven once appeared on the radio program *Kraft Music Hall*, for which he received $2,500 and a tray of various kinds of cheeses, courtesy of the sponsor. After receiving his payment, Mr. Niven wrote a check for $1,250, then cut the tray in half and presented Samuel Goldwyn with both the check and the half-tray of cheeses.[170]

• Chico Marx — the fake-Italian Marx Brother — was famous for his comedy. He was also famous for his gambling. He once bet movie director Leo McCarey $100 that he could throw a walnut further than him. Mr. McCarey agreed to the bet, and he picked a walnut from a bag of walnuts that Chico had and threw it. Chico then threw a walnut much further than Mr. McCarey and collected the $100. (Chico was not above cheating — he had earlier filled his walnut with lead.)[171]

• Early in his career, Hollywood director Frank Capra wanted to work for Mack Sennett, but he was unwilling to accept the $35-a-week starting salary that Mr. Sennett offered to everybody who was just beginning to work for him. Fortunately, Mr. Capra discovered a way out of the dilemma. He agreed to accept the $35-a-week starting salary — provided that Mr. Sennett give him a $10-a-week raise on his second day of work. Mr. Sennett accepted the compromise.[172]

• When French comic filmmaker Jacques Tati decided to entertain people in music halls, his father cut him off without a sou. No problem. Mr. Tati was able to get along well and happily without his father's money. When he needed a meal, he was able to go to a particular cabaret and entertain the customers by pretending to be a drunk waiter. In return, the proprietors of the cabaret were happy to give him a good meal and 50 francs.[173]

• When actor John Gilbert was high on the wheel of fortune, he lent many thousands of dollars to friends and acquaintances. When the wheel turned and he was nearly broke, he tried to call in his loans, but only Dorothy Parker repaid — promptly and in full. Mr. Gilbert sent her a basket of roses and a note reading "Thank you, Miss Finland." (Finland was the only country to repay its Great War debt to the United States.)[174]

• Filmmaker John Waters had little money when he started out, so he made many of his early films in coin-operated laundries and alleys. The coin-operated laundries were great sets because the lighting was wonderfully bright, and alleys had the big advantage of making it easy to run away when necessary.[175]

• While starring in a film in Hollywood, opera singer Helen Traubel met actor Walter Pidgeon. He told her, "Miss Traubel, I have all your records. You've cost me a lot of money." She replied, "So have you me. For all the movie tickets I've bought to see you."[176]

• While acting in her first film, *The Importance of Being Earnest*, Dorothy Tutin called for retake after retake. Finally, the producer asked if she knew how much a retake costs. After hearing the answer — £200 per minute — she stopped asking for retakes.[177]

• When Marilyn Monroe started making money as an actress, she opened a charge account at a store. But whereas most people would open their first charge account at a clothing store, she opened her first one at a bookstore.[178]

Mothers

• Hollywood director Jim Cruze bought his mother a fig farm, then hired men to buy her figs at outrageous prices. Once, someone offered to buy the fig farm from her. Mr. Cruze advised, "I wouldn't sell it — not when you get so much for your figs."[179]

• The child of actress Margaret Rutherford was a transsexual who went from being a man to being a woman. A wonderful mother, Margaret said about her child, "We loved him as a man, and now we'll love her as a woman."[180]

Music

• After Grace Moore became a movie star with *One Night of Love*, audiences at her music concerts began requesting song after song from the movie, including "Ciribiribin." While she was preparing a concert with conductor Willem Mengelberg, they looked at requests for songs for the upcoming concert. Over and over again, "Ciribiribin" was requested. This surprised Mr. Mengelberg, and he asked her what "Ciribiribin" was. She explained that it was an Italian folk song that was much too inconsequential to be sung with an orchestra and it was being requested because she had sung it in *One Night of Love*. Therefore, the two agreed to have her sing the song with only a piano providing accompaniment. However, at the concert the applause she received for this little song was so great that Mr. Mengelberg motioned for her to sing it again, and as she sang it various instruments from the orchestra joined in. After the concert, Mr. Mengelberg told her, "Regardless of who wrote that little song, where it came from, or whatever qualities it may have as a musical composition, if you in singing it can make an audience so happy, sing it until you die."[181]

• The movie *Star Wars* is 110 minutes long, and music plays for 90 of those minutes. Filmmaker George Lucas decided to have a musical theme for each of the major characters — the music for Darth Vader is very easily recognizable — and the character's theme plays when that character is on the screen. Mr. Lucas got the idea from the musical composition *Peter and the Wolf*, which has themes for each of its major characters.[182]

Names

• Hungarian producer Alexander Korda was the man who produced the film *The Third Man*, but after producer David O. Selznick bought the film for distribution in America, he put his name on it. One year later, Mr. Korda met Mr. Selznick and told him, "You know, David, I just hope I don't die before you." Mr. Selznick asked why, and Mr. Korda replied, "Because I hate to think of you going to

my gravestone, scratching off my name, and putting yours on instead."
[183]

• Jane Withers was a child actress who became famous because in the movie *Bright Eyes*, the character she played was mean to America's darling, Shirley Temple. Even before Jane was born, her mother wanted her to be a star. She decided to name her daughter "Jane" because she thought that "Withers" was a long name for a movie marquee, so a short first name was needed so the entire name would fit on the marquee.[184]

• When Luciano Pavarotti decided to make a movie, he met with the movie's producer to discuss the name his character should have. The meeting was held in Giorgio Fini's restaurant, and the food that day was cooked especially well — so well, in fact, that Mr. Pavarotti decided to name his character — with Mr. Fini's permission — Giorgio Fini. The movie was titled *Yes, Giorgio*.[185]

• Opera singer Helen Traubel knew a movie star who was very fond of talking about his famous friends. Once, a less famous actor walked by, and he said, "There, but for the grace of God, go I." Ms. Traubel's husband, Bill, murmured to her, "He's a name dropper."[186]

Politics

• When Michael Moore, director of *Roger and Me*, was in high school, the voting age was lowered to 18, so he called up the county clerk and asked, "Uh, I'm gonna be eighteen in a few weeks. If I can vote, does that mean I can also run for office?" It did, so he ran for school board on this platform: "Fire the high school principal and the assistant principal!" Of course, the adults got upset, so five of them ran against him. They split the anti-Michael vote, and young Michael was elected. The day after his political victory, he walked down the school hallway, with his shirt tail hanging out, and the principal said to him, "Good morning, Mr. Moore." Why did the principal call this high school student "Mr."? Because the high school student was now his boss.[187]

• Robert Redford starred in *The Candidate*, a movie about a naïve man running for the U.S. Senate without any idea of what he would do if he won the election. Instead of paying extras, the movie crew handed out to passersby political posters with Mr. Redford's face on them. When a crowd gathered, Mr. Redford appeared and acted. Sometimes people thought he was really running for office and so they would ask him questions. Someone once asked him, "What about Welfare?" Mr. Redford replied, "Beats me."[188]

• Groucho Marx once went on a goodwill tour to Mexico at a time when that country was politically unstable and its President changed frequently. After being told that his goodwill group would meet with the Mexican President the next day, Groucho asked, "What assurance have I got that he'll still be President by four o'clock tomorrow afternoon?"[189]

Practical Jokes

• Andre the Giant, who played Fezzik in the movie version of *The Princess Bride* by William Goldman, once was wrestling in Mexico while Arnold Schwarzenegger was in the audience. After winning the wrestling match, Andre gestured for Mr. Schwarzenegger to join him in the ring, then as the fans cheered and shouted, he told Mr. Schwarzenegger that he spoke Spanish and the fans were shouting for him to take his shirt off and strike some bodybuilding poses. Mr. Schwarzenegger happily obliged, then discovered later that Andre had been putting him on — the fans had NOT been shouting for him to take his shirt off and strike some bodybuilding poses.[190]

• Some practical jokes played on cartoonists found their way into actual cartoons. For example, Tex Avery, the man who created Bugs Bunny's personality, remembers a boy who worked in the mail room playing a practical joke on cartoon gagmen Friz Freleng and Tedd Pierce. The mail boy created a fake firecracker out of cardboard, painted it red and put a fuse on it, then he lit the fuse and threw the fake firecracker into the gag writers' room. Of course, they scattered, but nothing happened. The next time the mail boy threw something into the room, they remained seated and ignored it — of course, this time, the mail boy had thrown a real firecracker.[191]

• In 1952, Tex Avery created one of his most memorable gags in the cartoon "Magical Maestro." In the cartoon, a hair appeared to get caught in the projector and so was projected on screen. However, the cartoon character Poochini eventually notices the hair, stops singing, and removes the hair from the screen. This gag fooled many employees who ran the projectors. Some complained to MGM, which ordered that each film can containing the cartoon be labeled with a warning telling employees to ignore the hair, as it was part of the cartoon.[192]

• Hispanic movie star Antonio Banderas occasionally played practical jokes when he was a member of a traveling troupe of theatrical actors in his native Spain. For example, an actor on stage was required to eat a piece of bread, so Mr. Banderas put lots of salt and vinegar on the bread before it was taken on stage. However, being a member of this particular traveling troupe was not all fun and games. The actors put on plays that defied dictator Francesco Franco, so the actors, including Mr. Banderas, were sometimes arrested.[193]

• Margaret Lockwood is an English actress who appeared in *The Lady Vanishes*, which was directed by Alfred Hitchcock. Mr. Hitchcock enjoyed playing practical jokes; he once asked Ms. Lockwood to sit in a chair that had been wired so that it gave her an electric shock.[194]

Prejudice

• As a very out and very effeminate homosexual in London before the rise of the gay rights movement, Quentin Crisp was frequently beaten up, and he became as much of an expert in avoiding violent confrontations as one could become through experience. Once, some homophobes started following him, so he began to walk faster until a taxi appeared. He hailed the taxi and got into it. Frequently, confrontations would end at that point, but the young homophobes

surrounded the taxi and the taxi driver ordered Mr. Crisp to get out —
at other times, taxi drivers had driven slowly but persistently through
the crowd of homophobes. When Mr. Crisp was pulled out of the taxi,
the homophobes started to beat him and he fell to the ground. He was
afraid that they would start kicking him, but he managed to say, "I seem
to have annoyed you gentlemen in some way." This dignified sentence
was so unexpected that the homophobes let him get up and walk away,
although they continued to shout insults after him. Actor John Hurt
played Mr. Crisp in a celebrated 1975 made-for-TV movie titled *The
Naked Civil Servant*.[195]

• Hollywood screenwriter Charles Lederer was stationed in India
during World War II. While there, he accompanied a friend on a visit
to a British woman who vigorously denounced the Jews. This was a
mistake, because Mr. Lederer's father was a Jew, and Mr. Lederer was
known for his remarkable ability to get revenge on people who made
him angry. The British woman had a cabinet in her home, on top of
which a very expensive vase was displayed. Mr. Lederer stood by the
cabinet and asked, "What do you have against the Jews?" The British
woman insincerely replied, "Why, I have nothing against the Jews." Mr.
Lederer then smashed the very expensive vase and said, "You have now."
[196]

• Sometimes people who believe in racial stereotypes make
themselves look like the fools they are. Once, James "Jimmy" Wong
Howe, a famous Hollywood cinematographer, was preparing for the
opening of a Chinese restaurant he had invested in. He noticed a news
photographer trying to take a shot of the new restaurant despite being
in danger of being run over because he was standing in the street. Mr.
Howe told the photographer, "If you snap on a wide-angle lens, you can
move the camera up on the sidewalk." The photographer looked up at
Mr. Wong and said, "Look, Chinaman, let me take the pictures and you
go cook your noodles."[197]

• Groucho Marx and his wife looked for a beach club where their children could enjoy the ocean. However, Groucho was Jewish at a time when many clubs would not allow Jews to be members. When Groucho applied to become a member of a beach club, the manager said, "I don't know if you are aware of this, but we have a very restricted clientele here." Groucho knew that "restricted clientele" meant "no Jews allowed," so he mocked prejudice by telling the manager, "Look, Mister, I am Jewish. My wife is not Jewish. That means my kids are only half Jewish. Can't they go into the water up to their knees?"[198]

• Spike Lee's film *Do the Right Thing* is deliberately ambiguous. In it, a black man is unjustly killed, and in retaliation a mob of black people burns down a pizzeria owned by a white man. At its end, two quotations appear. The quotation by Martin Luther King preaches nonviolent resistance to injustice, while the quotation by Malcolm X says that violence in defense may be needed when blacks are attacked. When a reporter asked Mr. Lee what the right thing is, Mr. Lee replied, "I don't know. I know what the *wrong* thing is: racism."[199]

• Many of the top executives in the early days of Hollywood were Republicans. When Irving Thalberg's lawyer, Eddie Loeb, discovered that actor William Haines was a Democrat, he went straight to Mr. Thalberg and told him, "You know you have a Democratic snake here?" Fortunately, Mr. Thalberg, a Republican, was more enlightened than other Hollywood executives, so he replied, "The man's entitled to his own opinion," and he let Mr. Haines keep his job.[200]

• Peter Sellers, famous as Inspector Clouseau in Blake Edwards' Pink Panther movies, was Jewish, although not everyone realized that. Mary, the sister of comedian Terry-Thomas, met Peter in a hotel in Brighton, England, and told him that he would like it there, for among other attractions, no Jews were there. Mr. Sellers leaned across the table toward Mary, winked, and said, "Well, Mary, there is now!"[201]

• While filming *Hurry Sundown* in Louisiana in 1967, Jane Fonda was horrified to see prejudice at first hand. Black actors had leading roles in the movie, and this upset many white Louisiana residents. These prejudiced people objected to black actors using a motel pool, and they wrote threatening letters and slashed tires.[202]

• During the Civil Rights era, black comedian (and occasional movie actor) Dick Gregory put his career on the back burner so that he could participate in gaining rights for his people. When he was asked why he was practically giving up his career to do this, he replied, "They didn't laugh Hitler out of existence, did they?"[203]

• The famous Norwegian actress Liv Ullman was born in Tokyo. After she was born, the Japanese nurse told her mother, "I'm afraid it's a girl. Would you prefer to inform your husband yourself?"[204]

Chapter 5: From Preparation to Work

Preparation

• In 1977, Jane Fonda starred in the movie *Julia*, based on a friendship that playwright Lillian Hellman had when she was a young woman. To prepare for her role as the playwright, Ms. Fonda read half of a play that Ms. Hellman had written, then she set the play aside, pretended to be Ms. Hellman, and wrote the second half of the play. [205]

• Oprah Winfrey took seriously her role as Mattie in the television movie *The Women of Brewster Place*. To prepare for the role, she pretended to be Mattie and wrote a 200-page journal using the character's voice and point of view.[206]

Problem-Solving

• Early in his career, Harold Lloyd looked for a way to break into movies. He used to sit on a bench outside a film studio in hopes that he would be hired as an extra. As he waited, he noticed that many of the actors and extras walked out of the studio in their makeup to eat lunch, then they returned to the studio after their lunch break. Therefore, Mr. Lloyd put on makeup, and the movie studio guards, thinking that he was an actor, allowed him to enter the studio grounds along with the real actors. Inside the studio, Mr. Lloyd made some friends and started acting in films. He quickly became a famous silent-movie comedian and the star of such classic comedies as *Safety Last* and *The Freshman*. [207]

• In 1948, a year when a scandal could ruin an actor's career, Robert Mitchum was arrested for possession of marijuana. When he was asked what his career was, he replied, "Former actor." Newspaper articles about the arrest included the joke, and instead of having his career ruined, Mr. Mitchum found it enhanced. It also helped when articles included his answer to reporters who asked what life on a prison farm was like after spending 60 days there: "Just like Palm Springs —

without the riffraff, of course." (Mr. Mitchum continued to gain such publicity throughout his career. At Cannes, a young lady he was with took off the top of her bikini in front of photographers. Being a perfect gentleman, Mr. Mitchum preserved her modesty by covering her breasts — with his hands.)[208]

• When move producer Darryl F. Zanuck purchased the film rights of John Steinbeck's *Grapes of Wrath*, some people felt that he was buying the rights to prevent a movie ever being made of the book, which criticized banks and big farm interests. However, Mr. Zanuck did make a movie based on the book — the movie, starring Henry Fonda, is a classic. Because so many powerful people opposed the making of a movie based on *The Grapes of Wrath*, the making of the movie was kept secret. Whenever anyone asked which movie they were filming, they gave the title of another movie. In addition, Mr. Zanuck hired extra stagehands — that is, bodyguards — for the making of this particular film.[209]

• Anyone who has ever seen *Monty Python and the Holy Grail* knows that in the movie King Arthur and his knights do not ride horses; instead, they are followed by people using coconuts to make horse-riding noises. During the making of *Monty Python and the Holy Grail*, the budget was quite low and filming had to be completed in only five and a half weeks. In fact, the comedy troupe couldn't afford to use horses, which would have lengthened the time it took to make the movie. However, they managed to turn a weakness into a strength by substituting the use of coconuts for the horses.[210]

• In the film *The Seven Samurai*, some samurai are given a test. They are invited into a building where a man is hiding with a stick. The first samurai crosses the threshold, and the man hidden inside hits him with the stick. This samurai fails the test. Later, the second samurai crosses the threshold, dodges the blow, and hits the man who has the stick. This samurai also fails the test. Still later, the third samurai pauses at the threshold, studies the footprints in the dirt, and realizes that a man is hiding inside. This samurai passes the test.[211]

• Jack Palance excellently played a bad guy in the 1953 movie classic *Shane*. However, he was a bad horseman. After several tries, he made a perfect dismount, so director George Stevens used that shot in the movie every time Mr. Palance dismounted — and, by running the film backward, every time Mr. Palance mounted. In addition, in one scene Mr. Palance was supposed to gallop into town. But Mr. Palance was such a poor horseman, he finally was told to walk the horse into town. (This scene works very well in the movie.)[212]

• Mike Nichols directed the controversial film *Who's Afraid of Virginia Woolf?* Of course, the people behind the film worried that it would be censored by the Catholic Church's League of Decency, but Mr. Nichols came up with a plan to have the League approve it. He arranged for Jackie Kennedy to watch the movie while sitting beside the monsignor who headed the League and for Jackie to turn to the monsignor after the film ended and say, "How Jack would have loved it!" The plan worked; the League approved the film.[213]

• Early in his career, filmmaker John Waters and the actors in his films lived in cheap lodgings. However, they had no trouble getting repairs made. For example, when the heater conked out, Mr. Waters would simply telephone the landlord and say, "We know where you live, and since we don't have any heat, we'll be there tonight to stay with your family."[214]

• Movie crews sometimes have interesting assignments. When Fred Astaire's *Top Hat* was ready to film, Benito Mussolini controlled Italy, and the movie's producers knew that they could not get permission to film in Venice; therefore, they ordered the movie crew, "Build us Venice." They got what they wanted.[215]

• Action star Jackie Chan was injured during the filming of his action movie *Rumble in the Bronx*, so he had to wear a cast over his foot. No problem. Over the cast, Mr. Chan wore a sock that had been painted to resemble a tennis shoe and continued filming.[216]

• While filming the movie *The Flame of the Desert* in Egypt, opera singer Geraldine Farrar was so annoyed by the stink of a camel that each day she drenched it with perfume. This solved the problem, but at great expense.[217]

Screenplays

• Filmmaker George Lucas finds writing difficult. Early in his career, he wrote the script for his first feature, *THX 1138*, which was about a future dystopia. At one point, he looked at the draft and decided it was terrible. He showed it to a friend, Francis Ford Coppola, who read it and agreed that it was terrible: "It is. You're absolutely right." Nevertheless, he learned to write, and he created the screenplays (with some help from friends) for *American Graffiti* and *Star Wars*. [218]

• W.C. Fields used to take great delight in ripping off movie studios. He would write a script, then sell it to his movie studio for $25,000. The movie studio then would give the script back to him. However, because Mr. Fields had story approval, he would reject the script, then write another script and sell it to the studio for an additional $25,000.[219]

• Fred Astaire was very complimentary to the writers of his movies. Betty Comden and Adolph Green once read one of their scripts to him, and he said, "You can't ever top that. Nothing could ever be as good as that."[220]

Sex

• Marco Perella, a Texan actor, worked with Renée Zellweger before she made it big. One day, she wanted to play cards with Marco and three other men in a trailer during a break and because it was cold, she wanted to close the door of the trailer. Marco explained to sweet, innocent Renée that closing the door wasn't a good idea because of the gossip that was sure to be aroused. When Renée understood what

Marco was saying, she went to the door of the trailer and shouted, "ATTENTION, EVERYBODY! I JUST WANT EVERYONE TO KNOW THAT I'M CLOSING THIS DOOR SO WE CAN GET WARM, AND THAT DOESN'T MEAN WE'RE HAVING SEX! WE'RE PLAYING CARDS! WE'RE NOT SCREWING! NO HANKY-PANKY HERE! EVERYBODY, RELAX! NO SEX! NO SEX! NO SEX!" She then closed the door and said, "Deal."[221]

• Marilyn Monroe went to the Beverly Hills Hotel one morning to have breakfast with a friend, Nunnally Johnson. When the doorman rang Mr. Johnson's room to announce Ms. Monroe's presence, Mr. Johnson said, "Send her up." However, the doorman explained that it was hotel policy not to allow young ladies to visit gentlemen in their rooms. Mr. Johnson replied, "She isn't a young lady — she's a call girl. Send her up." The doorman sent her up.[222]

• Judy Holliday, star of *The Solid Gold Cadillac*, was a wonderful comedian, but she occasionally had to deal with sexual advances from studio executives. During one such episode, she reached into her dress, pulled out her falsies, handed them to the studio executive, and said, "Here. I think these are what you're after."[223]

Sound

• While making his very first movie, in the days in which sound equipment was unsophisticated, ventriloquist Edgar Bergen ran into a problem trying to get the sound of the voice of Charlie McCarthy, his dummy, onto the movie soundtrack. Eventually, the source of the problem was discovered to be a soundman who moved the microphone over to Charlie McCarthy whenever the dummy had a line.[224]

• The voice of the character Darth Vader in the *Star Wars* movies is menacing and easily recognizable — filmmaker George Lucas wanted the character, who has been badly burned and must stay in his costume to survive, to sound like a "walking iron lung." The voice was created by using a microphone inside a breathing regulator used by scuba divers. [225]

Special Effects

• For the movie *The Time Machine*, Wah Ming Chang and Gene Warren needed to show a volcano erupting and its lava flowing through a town. Therefore, they created a miniature town and cooked 250 gallons of red-colored oatmeal to represent the lava. Unfortunately, they cooked the oatmeal on Friday and did the filming on Monday. Only after pouring the containers on the set during filming did they discover that the oatmeal had spoiled. The special effects room was so small that Mr. Chang and Mr. Warren found themselves pinned to a wall by 250 gallons of stinking, spoiled oatmeal. Nevertheless, they eventually filmed the scene correctly and ended up winning two Oscars for their special effects in *The Time Machine*.[226]

• In Steven Spielberg's movie *Jaws*, he used a huge mechanical shark. During one scene in which Richard Dreyfuss' character goes underwater in a protective cage, Mr. Spielberg used a real great white shark. The real shark was much smaller than the mechanical shark, so to make the shark appear as big as the mechanical shark, Mr. Spielberg used a little person (aka midget or dwarf) to stand in for Mr. Dreyfuss in the scene.[227]

Stars

• When *Psycho* was first released, director Alfred Hitchcock ordered that no audience member be admitted after the film began. The audience assumed that something shocking would happen right away, although the film begins slowly. Actually, Mr. Hitchcock was doing something radically different — killing off the big star, Janet Leigh, early in the film. Mr. Hitchcock didn't want members of the audience to arrive late, then keep wondering when Ms. Leigh was going to appear on screen.[228]

• Once a star, always a star. When she was in her 70s, child star Shirley Temple showed up for a *People* magazine photo shoot featuring breast cancer survivors. She announced, "I want to be in the middle of the shot because that's the star position. They can't cut you out if you're in the middle." All of the other people in the photo shoot were happy to give her the star position.[229]

Telegrams

• Peter Lorre was an excellent actor who became renowned for his performance as a child murderer in Fritz Lang's film *M*. Because he was Jewish, he left Germany at the beginning of the Nazis' rise to power and moved to Vienna. Nazi propagandist Paul Joseph Goebbels did not know that Mr. Lorre was Jewish and asked him to come back to Germany. Mr. Lorre replied with this telegram: "THERE ISN'T ROOM IN GERMANY FOR TWO MURDERERS LIKE HITLER AND ME."[230]

• The production costs were mounting for the movie *The Captain Hates the Sea*, starring the noted actors — and drinkers — John Gilbert and Victor McLaglen, so Columbia Studios head Harry Cohn sent the director, Lewis Milestone, this telegram: "HURRY UP! THE COST IS STAGGERING!" Mr. Milestone sent back this telegram: "SO IS THE CAST."[231]

Telephones

• W.C. Fields didn't care for Hollywood studio bigshots. Once, Louis B. Mayer called him. Mr. Fields' friend, Corey Ford, answered the telephone and told him that Mr. Mayer was wondering why Mr. Fields hadn't shown up for filming that day. Mr. Fields said, "Give him an evasive answer. Something on the order of 'Drop dead.'" (When Mr. Fields died, humorist Frank Sullivan sent this telegram to one of Mr. Fields' friends: "I HOPE HE GIVES ST. PETER AN EVASIVE ANSWER.")[232]

• While making the 1948 movie *Foreign Affair*, actress Jean Arthur worried that director Billy Wilder was giving the best close-ups not to herself, but to her co-star, Marlene Dietrich. Forty-five years later, Ms. Arthur gave Mr. Wilder a telephone call. She had just seen the movie on television and wanted to apologize.[233]

• While making a motion picture, comedian Jack Oakie did not show up to work one day. The cast, crew, and director all were waiting for him in the hot sun. Mr. Oakie telephoned them. He said, "Guess where I am?" — then hung up.[234]

• Comedian Bob Hope had clout. He once telephoned a movie theater in Palm Springs to ask when the movie started. The person who answered the telephone replied, "Mr. Hope, what time would you like it to start?"[235]

Tobacco

• Hugh Herbert played comic support in movies of the 1930s and 1940s. He was also funny in real life. One day, insult comedian Jack E. Leonard saw Mr. Herbert smoking a cigar — from which clouds of smoke were billowing — at the Friars Club and asked him, "Don't you ever inhale?" Mr. Herbert replied, "Not with you in the room."[236]

• Movie director John Waters once decided to use aversion therapy to get himself to quit smoking, so he ate all the butts in an ashtray. Unfortunately, he decided that they really didn't taste that bad, and he kept on smoking.[237]

Work

• While working at RKO, Lucille Ball had a notable encounter with movie star Katherine Hepburn. Lucy was having some studio portraits taken, and since she wanted to look her best, she went to Ms. Hepburn's makeup man and talked him into making her up. All went well until Ms. Hepburn was announced and Lucy was thrown out of the makeup room. Suddenly she realized that she had left her tooth caps in the makeup room — an unfortunate event because you can't take a glamour portrait with bad teeth. She tried to catch the make-up man's attention through a small window, but he didn't see her, so finally an angry Lucy threw a cup of coffee at him, missing him, but hitting Ms. Hepburn. Ms. Hepburn didn't say anything to Lucy, but she got up and left the studio, saying she couldn't work that day.[238]

• While making the movie *Shampoo*, Warren Beatty had to ride a motorcycle around a corner, where he met Jack Warden coming the other way in a Mercedes. The two vehicles nearly collided, and Mr. Beatty put the motorcycle on the ground. A stagehand named Ron Webber came over to help him, and Mr. Beatty accidentally kicked the motorcycle into him, burning Mr. Webber's arm without meaning to and without knowing he had burned it. The next day, Mr. Beatty saw the burn and asked Mr. Webber how he had gotten it. Mr. Webber replied, "Hey, man, you kicked that d*mn bike into me and burnt my arm." Mr. Beatty then said, "Ron, from now on, you're in all my films." He kept his word — every time he made a film, he hired Mr. Webber. [239]

• Al Boasberg was a wonderful comedy writer, but he didn't like to be rushed. Once, producer Irving Thalberg rushed him. Mr. Thalberg wanted a scene written for the Marx Brothers — now. Finally, Mr. Boasberg said that he had written the material that Mr. Thalberg wanted. Then he told Mr. Thalberg that he was leaving his office, but would leave the scene behind. The Marx Brothers and Mr. Thalberg rushed to Mr. Boasberg's office to read the scene — and found it cut into many pieces and nailed to the ceiling. According to Groucho, "It took us about five hours to piece it together." But the scene was worth all that work — Mr. Boasberg had written what eventually became the famous scene in *A Night at the Opera* in which many, many people crowd into a small room.[240]

• Being a successful actress can be very difficult work. While filming the movie *Scream 2*, Sarah Michelle Gellar was also starring in TV's *Buffy the Vampire Slayer*. For a while, she worked on the TV series Monday through Thursday, then worked on *Scream 2* Friday through Sunday. Sometimes, she would work on *Buffy* until 2 a.m., then show up in three hours at 5 a.m. to start another workday. One morning, Sarah was driving to work with the controvertible top of her car down. She noticed people staring at her, then looked down and saw that she was only partially dressed — she was so tired that she had forgotten to put on a dress.[241]

• Famous cartoonist Chuck Jones' father failed time after time as a businessman, but this turned out to have an advantage for Chuck and his siblings. When his father started a new company, he would buy lots of business stationery with the company's name and letterhead on it, and lots of pencils, also with the company's name on them. When the business failed, Chuck and his siblings had lots of paper and pencils to draw with. Chuck said, "We Joneses were rolling in tons of lovely white bond paper." As an adult, Mr. Jones worked on cartoons featuring Wile E. Coyote, Bugs Bunny, Daffy Duck, and other Looney Tunes characters.[242]

• Charles Lederer became a famous screenwriter in Hollywood, but in early life he seldom worked. Instead, he slept until noon and spent a lot of time in swimming pools. This was something that his girlfriend didn't like, so she took him out to eat at the Colony Restaurant, where she encouraged him to stop loafing and to find work, etc. Mr. Lederer listened to everything that his girlfriend had to say to him, then he stood up, took off his pants, and handed them to her, saying, "Here, you wear them." Then he walked out of the restaurant. [243]

• Comedian Joe E. Brown's father was a house painter who took pride in his work. One day he was taking his son to a baseball game when they passed a house he had painted a few weeks before. However, as he looked at the house he noticed a spot on the porch that he had forgotten to paint, so the baseball game had to wait until he got some paint and finished the job. Mr. Brown writes, "I was a grown man before I realized examples such as this were the foundation of my desire to give my best in every job."[244]

• Tex Avery, the director of many classic Bugs Bunny cartoons and the man who gave Bugs his distinctive personality, was a perfectionist who worked long hours to make his cartoons funny. In fact, he once worked so hard that he delayed urinating for so long that he ended up in a hospital, where a catheter had to be used to empty his overfull bladder. Despite his hard work, he was insecure about his job, and when he was away from his desk he carried around a timing chart for cartoons so it always looked as if he were working.[245]

• A popular low-brow comedy series in Great Britain was the *Carry On* series of films. Between 1958 and 1992, 31 movies were made in the series, beginning with *Carry On Sergeant* and ending with *Carry On Columbus*. *Carry On* creators and creative team Peter Rogers and Gerald Thomas were sometimes asked what project they were working on — they always replied, "Same film, different title."[246]

• When Carol Burnett was growing up, she worked part-time at a movie theater that broadcast the sound of the movie into the area she staffed. She never saw the movie *Ivanhoe*, but she did hear it more than a hundred times. Decades afterward, she could still repeat verbatim long passages from the movie.[247]

• At one time, Whoopi Goldberg, Academy Award-winning actress of *Ghost*, worked at a mortuary, where she applied makeup to corpses and dressed their hair. According to Ms. Goldberg, this was "great work" because she was "tired of working on living people who *all* wanted to look like Farrah Fawcett."[248]

• According to Michael Moore, the director of *Roger and Me*, once a year factory workers in Flint, Michigan, dress up in white shirts (instead of their usual blue shirts) as a visual reminder that the bosses "are no better than anyone else."[249]

• As a comic filmmaker, Jacques Tati carefully observed people. On a street one day, he looked at three people arguing about how much a cabbage cost. When his companion asked what he was doing, he replied, "Working."[250]

Appendix A: Bibliography

Adamson, Joe. *Tex Avery: King of Cartoons*. New York: Da Capo Press, Inc., 1985.

Adler, Bill. *Fred Astaire: A Wonderful Life*. New York: Carroll & Graf Publishers, Inc., 1987.

Allison, Amy. *Antonio Banderas*. Philadelphia, PA: Chelsea House Publishers, 2001.

Bailey, Paul, editor. *The Stately Homo: A Celebration of the Life of Quentin Crisp*. London: Bantam Press, 2000.

Bernotas, Bob. *Spike Lee: Filmmaker*. Hillside, NJ: Enslow Publications, Inc., 1993.

Bessette, Roland L. *Mario Lanza: Tenor in Exile*. Portland, OR: Amadeus Press, 1999.

Bogdanovich, Peter. *Peter Bogdanovich's Movie of the Week*. New York: Ballantine Books, 1999.

Bonvicini, Candido. *The Tenor's Son: My Days With Pavarotti*. New York: St. Martin's Press, 1992.

Boo, Michael. *The Story of Figure Skating*. New York: William Morrow and Company, 1998.

Briggs, Joe Bob. *Profoundly Disturbing: Shocking Movies That Changed History!* New York: Universe Books, 2003.

Bronski, Michael, consulting editor. *Outstanding Lives: Profiles of Lesbians and Gay Men*. Foreword by Jewelle L. Gomez; Christa Brelin and Michael J. Tyrkus, editors. Detroit, MI: Visible Ink Press, 1997.

Brown, David. *Star Billing: Tell-Tale Trivia from Hollywood*. London: Weidenfeld and Nicolson, Limited, 1985.

Brown, Joe E. *Laughter is a Wonderful Thing*. As told to Ralph Hancock. New York: A.S. Barnes and Co., 1956.

Bryan III, J. *Merry Gentlemen (and One Lady)*. New York: Atheneum, 1985.

Burton, Hal, editor. *Acting in the Sixties*. London: British Broadcasting Corporation, 1970.

Campbell, Bruce. *If Chins Could Kill: Confessions of a B Movie Actor*. New York: Thomas Dunne Books, 2001.

Canemaker, John. *Tex Avery: The MGM Years, 1942-1955*. Atlanta, GA: Turner Publishing, Inc., 1996.

Cantor, Eddie. *As I Remember Them*. New York: Duell, Sloan and Pearce, 1963. (Mr. Cantor's collaborator for most of these pieces was Vivian M. Bowes, to whom he gives credit on the acknowledgements page.)

Cantor, Eddie. *Take My Life*. Written with Jane Kesner Ardmore. Garden City, NY: Doubleday, 1957.

Caper, William. *Whoopi Goldberg: Comedian and Movie Star*. Springfield, NJ: Enslow Publications, Inc., 1999.

Clercq, Tanaquil Le. *The Ballet Cook Book*. New York: Stein and Day, Publishers, 1966.

Cowan, Lore and Maurice. *The Wit of the Jews*. Nashville, TN: Aurora Publishers, Limited, 1970.

Chapman, Graham. *Graham Crackers*. Compiled by Jim Yoakum. Franklin Lakes, NJ: Career Press, Inc., 1997.

Cranston, Toller. *Zero Tollerance*. With Martha Lowder Kimball. Toronto, Canada: McClelland and Stewart, Inc., 1997.

Crowl, Samuel. *Shakespeare at the Cineplex: The Kenneth Branagh Era*. Athens, OH: Ohio University Press, 2003.

Current Biography Yearbook. New York: H.W. Wilson Company.

David, Jay. *The Life and Humor of Robin Williams*. New York: William Morrow and Company, Inc., 1999.

De Angelis, Therese. *Jodie Foster*. Philadelphia, PA: Chelsea House Publishers, 2001.

dePaola, Tomie. *26 Fairmount Avenue*. New York: G.P. Putnam's Sons, 1999.

dePaola, Tomie. *Things Will NEVER Be the Same*. New York: G.P. Putnam's Sons, 2003.

Diamond, Arthur. *Charlie Chaplin*. San Diego, CA: Lucent Books, 1995.

Diller, Phyllis. *Like a Lampshade in a Whorehouse: My Life in Comedy*. With Richard Buskin. London: Penguin Group, 2005.

Edelson, Edward. *Funny Men of the Movies*. New York: Pocket Books, 1976.

Epstein, Lawrence J. *The Haunted Smile: The Story of Jewish Comedians in America*. New York: PublicAffairs, 2001.

Epstein, Lawrence J. *Mixed Nuts: America's Love Affair with Comedy Teams From Burns and Allen to Belushi and Aykroyd*. New York: PublicAffairs, 2004.

Erlanger, Ellen. *Jane Fonda: More Than a Movie Star*. Minneapolis, MN: Lerner Publications Company, 1984.

Farrar, Geraldine. *Such Sweet Compulsion*. New York: The Greystone Press, 1938.

Feather, Leonard, and Jack Tracy. *Laughter from the Hip: The Lighter Side of Jazz*. New York: Da Capo Press, Inc., 1979.

Fleming, Peggy. *The Long Program*. With Peter Kaminsky. New York: Pocket Books, 1999.

Ford, Corey. *The Time of Laughter*. Boston, MA: Little, Brown and Company, 1967.

Ford, Michael Thomas. *Alec Baldwin Doesn't Love Me, and Other Trials from My Queer Life*. Los Angeles, CA: Alyson Books, 1998.

Ford, Michael Thomas. *It's Not Mean If It's True*. Los Angeles, CA: Alyson Books, 2000.

Fox, Patty. *Star Style: Hollywood Legends as Fashion Icons*. Santa Monica, CA: Angel City Press, Inc., 1995.

Frank, Rusty E. *Tap! The Greatest Tap Dance Stars and Their Stories, 1900-1955*. New York: William Morrow and Company, Inc., 1990.

Fremon, David K. *The Great Depression in American History*. Springfield, NJ: Enslow Publications, Inc., 1997.

Galas, Judith C. *Gay Rights*. San Diego, CA: Lucent Books, 1996.

Garner, Joe. *Now Showing: Unforgettable Moments from the Movies*. Kansas City, MO: Andrews McMeel Publishing, 2003.

Giles, Sarah. *Fred Astaire: His Friends Talk*. New York: Doubleday, 1988.

Gilliatt, Penelope. *Jacques Tati*. London: The Woburn Press, 1976.

Gingras, Angele de T. *From Bussing to Bugging: The Best in Congressional Humor*. Washington, D.C.: Acropolis Books, Limited, 1973.

Goldman, William. *The Princess Bride*. New York: Ballantine Books, 2003.

Gonzales, Doreen. *AIDS: Ten Stories of Courage*. Springfield, NJ: Enslow Publications, Inc., 1996.

Guttmacher, Peter. *Legendary Comedies*. New York: MetroBooks, 1996.

Hadleigh, Boze. *Hollywood Gays*. New York: Barricade Books, Inc., 1996.

Halliwell, Leslie. *The Filmgoer's Book of Quotes*. New Rochelle, NY: Arlington House, Publishers, 1973.

Harris, Nick. *I Wish I'd Said That!* London: Octopus Books, Limited, 1984.

Haskins, Jim, and N.R. Mitgang. *Mr. Bojangles: The Story of Bill Robinson*. New York: William Morrow and Company, Inc., 1988.

Havens, Candace. *Joss Whedon: The Genius Behind Buffy*. Dallas, TX: BenBella Books, 2003.

Hay, Peter. *Movie Anecdotes*. New York: Oxford University Press, 1990.

Hecht, Andrew. *Hollywood Merry-Go-Round*. New York: Grosset and Dunlap, Publishers, 1947.

Henry, Lewis C. *Humorous Anecdotes About Famous People*. Garden City, NY: Halcyon House, 1948.

Hope, Bob. *The Road to Hollywood: My Forty-Year Love Affair With the Movies*. With Bob Thomas. Garden City, NY: Doubleday & Company, Inc., 1977.

Hyams, Joe. *Zen in the Martial Arts*. New York: Bantam Books, 1979.

Jacobsen, Peter. *Embedded Balls*. With Jack Sheehan. New York: G.P. Putnam's Sons, 2005.

Kline, Sally, editor. *George Lucas: Interviews*. Jackson, MI: University Press of Mississippi, 1999.

Krohn, Katherine E. *Marilyn Monroe: Norma Jeane's Dream*. Minneapolis, MN: Lerner Publications Company, 1997.

Leonard, Sheldon. *And the Show Goes On: Broadway and Hollywood Adventures*. New York: Limelight, 1994.

Linkletter, Art. *Oops! Or, Life's Awful Moments*. Garden City, NY: Doubleday & Company, Inc., 1967.

Lipman, Steve. *Laughter in Hell: The Use of Humor during the Holocaust*. Northvale, NJ: Jason Aronson, Inc., 1991.

Mabery, D.L. *George Lucas*. Minneapolis, MN: Lerner Publications Company, 1987.

Malone, Mary. *Will Rogers: Cowboy Philosopher*. Springfield, NJ: Enslow Publications, Inc., 1996.

Maltin, Leonard. *The Great Movie Comedians: From Charlie Chaplin to Woody Allen*. New York: Crown Publishers, Inc., 1978.

Maltin, Leonard. *Movie Comedy Teams*. New York: The New American Library, Inc., 1970.

Manchel, Frank. *The Rise of Film Comedy*. New York: Franklin Watts, Inc., 1973.

Martin, W.K. *Marlene Dietrich*. New York: Chelsea House, 1995.

Marx, Arthur. *Life With Groucho*. New York: Simon and Schuster, 1954.

Marx, Arthur. *Son of Groucho*. New York: David McKay Company, Inc., 1972.

Marx, Groucho. *Groucho and Me*. New York: Bernard Geis Associates, 1959.

Maychick, Diana. *Audrey Hepburn*. New York: Carol Publishing Co., 1993.

Meyer, Miriam Weiss, Project Editor. *Top Picks: People*. Pleasantville, NY: Reader's Digest Educational Division, 1977.

Miller, John. *Ralph Richardson: The Authorized Biography*. London: Sidgwick and Jackson, 1995.

Moore, Grace. *You're Only Human Once*. Garden City, NY: Doubleday, Doran and Co., Inc., 1944.

Moore, Michael. *Downsize This!* New York: HarperPerennial, 1997.

Moore, Michael. *Stupid White Men*. New York: HarperCollins, Publishers, Inc., 2001.

Morella, Joe, and Edward Z. Epstein. *Forever Lucy*. New York: Berkley Books, 1990.

Morgan, David. *Monty Python Speaks*. New York: Avon Books, Inc., 1999.

Morley, Robert. *Around the World in Eighty-One Years*. London: Hodder & Stoughton, 1990.

Morley, Robert. *Robert Morley's Book of Bricks*. New York: G.P. Putnam's Sons, 1979.

Muir, John Kenneth. *An Askew View*. New York: Applause Theatre and Cinema Books, 2002.

Nachman, Gerald. *Seriously Funny: The Rebel Comedians of the 1950s and 1960s*. New York: Pantheon Books, 2003.

Nash, Bruce, and Allan Zullo. *The Hollywood Walk of Shame*. Compiled by Martha Moffett. Kansas City, MO: Andrews and McMeel, 1993.

Oakie, Victoria Horne, compiler and editor. *"Dear Jack": Hollywood Birthday Reminiscences to Jack Oakie*. Portland, OR: Strawberry Hill Press, 1994.

Parker, Jessica. *Great African Americans in Film*. New York: Crabtree Publishing Company, 1997.

Parla, Paul, and Charles P. Mitchell. *Screen Sirens Scream!* Jefferson, NC, and London: McFarland and Company, Inc., Publishers, 2000.

Perella, Marco. *Adventures of a No Name Actor*. New York: Bloomsbury, 2002.

Powers, Tom. *Horror Movies*. Minneapolis, MN: Lerner Publications Company, 1989.

Powers, Tom. *Movie Monsters*. Minneapolis, MN: Lerner Publications Company, 1989.

Price, Vincent. *The Book of Joe*. Garden City, NY: Doubleday & Co., Inc., 1961.

Primack, Ben, adapter and editor. *The Ben Hecht Show: Impolitic Observations from the Freest Thinker of 1950s Television*. Jefferson, NC: McFarland & Company, Inc., Publishers, 1993.

Rigg, Diana, compiler. *No Turn Unstoned: The Worst Ever Theatrical Reviews*. Los Angeles, CA: Silman-James Press, 1982.

Riley, Gail Blasser. *Wah Ming Chang: Artist and Master of Special Effects*. Springfield, NJ: Enslow Publications, Inc., 1995.

Rockwell, Bart. *World's Strangest Basketball Stories*. Mahwah, NJ: Watermill Press, 1993.

Rowell, Edward K., editor. *Humor for Preaching and Teaching*. Grand Rapids, MI: Baker Books, 1996.

Russell, Mark, editor. *Out of Character*. New York: Bantam Books, 1997.

Sante, Luc, and Melissa Holbrook Pierson, editors. *O.K. You Mugs: Writers on Movie Actors*. New York: Pantheon Books, 1999.

Schafer, Kermit. *The Bedside Book of Celebrity Bloopers*. New York: Crown Publishers, Inc., 1984.

Schuman, Michael A. *Halle Berry: "Beauty is Not Merely Physical."* Berkeley Heights, NJ: Enslow Publishers, Inc., 2006.

Silverman, Stephen M. *Funny Ladies: The Women Who Make Us Laugh*. New York: Harry N. Abrams, Inc., 1999.

Smith, H. Allen. *Lost in the Horse Latitudes*. Garden City, NY: Doubleday, Doran, and Co., 1944.

Smith, H. Allen. *Low Man on a Totem Pole*. Garden City, NY: Doubleday, Doran and Co., Inc., 1941.

Smith, Ron. *Comic Support*. New York: Carol Publishing Group, 1993.

Sobol, Donald J. *Encyclopedia Brown's Book of the Wacky Outdoors*. New York: William Morrow and Company, Inc., 1987.

Sorel, Nancy Caldwell, and Edward Sorel. *First Encounters: A Book of Memorable Meetings*. New York: Alfred A. Knopf, 1994.

Steffens, Bradley, and Robyn M. Weaver. *Cartoonists*. San Diego, CA: Lucent Books, 2000.

Stone, Laurie. *Laughing in the Dark: A Decade of Subversive Comedy*. Hopewell, NJ: The Ecco Press, 1997.

Tanitch, Robert, deviser and compiler. *Ralph Richardson: A Tribute*. London: Evans Brothers, Limited, 1982.

Taylor, Glenhall. *Before Television: The Radio Years*. New York: A.S. Barnes and Company, 1979.

Taylor, Robert Lewis. *W.C. Fields: His Follies and Fortunes*. Garden City, NY: Doubleday and Company, Inc., 1949.

Telushkin, Rabbi Joseph. *Jewish Wisdom: Ethical, Spiritual, and Historical Lessons from the Great Works and Thinkers*. New York: William Morrow and Company, Inc., 1994.

Terry-Thomas, and Terry Daum. *Terry-Thomas ... Tells Tales*. London: Robson Books, 1990.

Tevis, Jamie Griggs. *My Life with the Hustler*. Athens, OH: The Author, 2003.

Took, Barry. *Comedy Greats: A Celebration of Comic Genius Past and Present*. Wellingborough, Northamptonshire, England: Equation, 1989.

Tracy, Kathleen. *The Girl's Got Bite*. New York: St. Martin's Press, 2003.

Traubel, Helen. *St. Louis Woman*. New York: Duell, Sloan and Pearce, 1959.

Tully, Jim. *A Dozen and One*. Hollywood, CA: Murray & Gee, Inc., Publishers, 1943.

Vilanch, Bruce. *Bruce! Adventures in the Skin Trade and Other Essays*. New York: Jeremy P. Tarcher/Putnam, 2000.

Wagenknecht, Edward. *Seven Daughters of the Theater*. Norman, OK: University of Oklahoma Press, 1964.

Waters, John. *Crackpot: The Obsessions of John Waters*. New York: Vintage Books, 1987.

Waters, John. *Shock Value*. New York: Dell Publishing Company, Inc., 1981.

Weintraub, Joseph, editor. *The Wit and Wisdom of Mae West*. New York: G.P. Putnam's Sons, 1967.

Wellman, Sam. *Ben Affleck*. Philadelphia, PA: Chelsea House Publishers, 2000.

White, Betty. *Here We Go Again: My Life in Television*. New York: St. Martin's Press, 1995.

Williams, John A., and Dennis A. Williams. *If I Stop, I'll Die: The Comedy and Tragedy of Richard Pryor*. New York: Thunder's Mouth Press, 1991.

Williams, Kenneth. *Acid Drops*. London: J.M. Dent & Sons, Ltd., 1980.

Wooten, Sara McIntosh. *Oprah Winfrey: Talk Show Legend*. Berkeley Heights, NJ: Enslow Publications, Inc., 1999.

Worland, Bill. *"Fumble Four Bars In."* London: Minerva Press, 1996.

Zimmerman, Paul D., and Burt Goldblatt. *The Marx Brothers at the Movies*. New York: G.P. Putnam's Sons, 1968.

Appendix B: About the Author

It was a dark and stormy night. Suddenly a cry rang out, and on a hot summer night in 1954, Josephine, wife of Carl Bruce, gave birth to a boy — me. Unfortunately, this young married couple allowed Reuben Saturday, Josephine's brother, to name their first-born. Reuben, aka "The Joker," decided that Bruce was a nice name, so he decided to name me Bruce Bruce. I have gone by my middle name — David — ever since.

Being named Bruce David Bruce hasn't been all bad. Bank tellers remember me very quickly, so I don't often have to show an ID. It can be fun in charades, also. When I was a counselor as a teenager at Camp Echoing Hills in Warsaw, Ohio, a fellow counselor gave the signs for "sounds like" and "two words," then she pointed to a bruise on her leg twice. Bruise Bruise? Oh, yeah, Bruce Bruce is the answer!

Uncle Reuben, by the way, gave me a haircut when I was in kindergarten. He cut my hair short and shaved a small bald spot on the back of my head. My mother wouldn't let me go to school until the bald spot grew out again.

Of all my brothers and sisters (six in all), I am the only transplant to Athens, Ohio. I was born in Newark, Ohio, and have lived all around Southeastern Ohio. However, I moved to Athens to go to Ohio University and have never left.

At Ohio U, I never could make up my mind whether to major in English or Philosophy, so I got a bachelor's degree with a double major in both areas, then I added a Master of Arts degree in English and a Master of Arts degree in Philosophy. Yes, I have my MAMA degree.

Currently, and for a long time to come (I eat fruits and veggies), I am spending my retirement writing books such as *Nadia Comaneci: Perfect 10*, *The Funniest People in Comedy*, *Homer's* Iliad: *A Retelling in Prose*, and *William Shakespeare's* Hamlet: *A Retelling in Prose.*

If all goes well, I will publish one or two books a year for the rest of my life. (On the other hand, a good way to make God laugh is to tell Her your plans.)

Appendix C: Some Books by David Bruce

Anecdote Collections

250 Anecdotes About Opera
250 Anecdotes About Religion
250 Anecdotes About Religion: Volume 2
250 Music Anecdotes
Be a Work of Art: 250 Anecdotes and Stories
Cool and Funny People: 250 Anecdotes and Stories
The Coolest People in Art: 250 Anecdotes
The Coolest People in the Arts: 250 Anecdotes
The Coolest People in Books: 250 Anecdotes
The Coolest People in Comedy: 250 Anecdotes
The Coolest People in the Performing Arts: 250 Anecdotes
Create, Then Take a Break: 250 Anecdotes
Dance, Music, Theater: 250m Anecdotes and Stories
Don't Fear the Reaper: 250 Anecdotes
The Funniest People in Art: 250 Anecdotes
The Funniest People in Books: 250 Anecdotes
The Funniest People in Books, Volume 2: 250 Anecdotes
The Funniest People in Books, Volume 3: 250 Anecdotes
The Funniest People in Comedy: 250 Anecdotes
The Funniest People in Dance: 250 Anecdotes
The Funniest People in Families: 250 Anecdotes
The Funniest People in Families, Volume 2: 250 Anecdotes
The Funniest People in Families, Volume 3: 250 Anecdotes
The Funniest People in Families, Volume 4: 250 Anecdotes
The Funniest People in Families, Volume 5: 250 Anecdotes
The Funniest People in Families, Volume 6: 250 Anecdotes
The Funniest People in Movies: 250 Anecdotes
The Funniest People in Music: 250 Anecdotes
The Funniest People in Music, Volume 2: 250 Anecdotes
The Funniest People in Music, Volume 3: 250 Anecdotes
The Funniest People in Neighborhoods: 250 Anecdotes
The Funniest People in Relationships: 250 Anecdotes
The Funniest People in Sports: 250 Anecdotes

The Funniest People in Sports, Volume 2: 250 Anecdotes
The Funniest People in Television and Radio: 250 Anecdotes
The Funniest People in Theater: 250 Anecdotes
The Funniest People Who Live Life: 250 Anecdotes
The Funniest People Who Live Life, Volume 2: 250 Anecdotes
History and Politics: 250 Stories
The Kindest People Who Do Good Deeds, Volume 1: 250 Anecdotes
The Kindest People Who Do Good Deeds, Volume 2: 250 Anecdotes
The Kindest People Who Do Good Deeds, Volume 3: 250 Anecdotes
The Kindest People Who Do Good Deeds, Volume 4: 250 Anecdotes
The Kindest People Who Do Good Deeds, Volume 5: 250 Anecdotes
Life is Good: 250 Anecdotes and Stories
Maximum Cool: 250 Anecdotes
The Most Interesting People in Movies: 250 Anecdotes
The Most Interesting People in Politics and History: 250 Anecdotes
The Most Interesting People in Politics and History, Volume 2: 250 Anecdotes
The Most Interesting People in Politics and History, Volume 3: 250 Anecdotes
The Most Interesting People in Religion: 250 Anecdotes
The Most Interesting People in Sports: 250 Anecdotes
The Most Interesting People Who Live Life: 250 Anecdotes
The Most Interesting People Who Live Life, Volume 2: 250 Anecdotes
Movies, Radio, and Television: 250 Anecdotes
Reality is Fabulous: 250 Anecdotes and Stories
Resist Psychic Death: 250 Anecdotes
Science and Religion: 250 Anecdotes and Stories
Seize the Day: 250 Anecdotes and Stories

Retellings of a Classic Work of Literature

Arden of Faversham: *A Retelling*
Ben Jonson's The Alchemist: *A Retelling*
Ben Jonson's The Arraignment, or Poetaster: *A Retelling*
Ben Jonson's Bartholomew Fair: *A Retelling*
Ben Jonson's The Case is Altered: *A Retelling*
Ben Jonson's Catiline's Conspiracy: *A Retelling*
Ben Jonson's The Devil is an Ass: *A Retelling*
Ben Jonson's Epicene: *A Retelling*
Ben Jonson's Every Man in His Humor: *A Retelling*
Ben Jonson's Every Man Out of His Humor: *A Retelling*
Ben Jonson's The Fountain of Self-Love, or Cynthia's Revels: *A Retelling*
Ben Jonson's The Magnetic Lady, or Humors Reconciled: *A Retelling*

Ben Jonson's The New Inn, or The Light Heart: *A Retelling*

Ben Jonson's Sejanus' Fall: *A Retelling*

Ben Jonson's The Staple of News: *A Retelling*

Ben Jonson's A Tale of a Tub: *A Retelling*

Ben Jonson's Volpone, or the Fox: *A Retelling*

Christopher Marlowe's Complete Plays: Retellings

Christopher Marlowe's Dido, Queen of Carthage: *A Retelling*

Christopher Marlowe's Doctor Faustus: *Retellings of the 1604 A-Text and of the 1616 B-Text*

Christopher Marlowe's Edward II: *A Retelling*

Christopher Marlowe's The Massacre at Paris: *A Retelling*

Christopher Marlowe's The Rich Jew of Malta: *A Retelling*

Christopher Marlowe's Tamburlaine, Parts 1 and 2: *Retellings*

Dante's Divine Comedy: *A Retelling in Prose*

Dante's Inferno: *A Retelling in Prose*

Dante's Purgatory: *A Retelling in Prose*

Dante's Paradise: *A Retelling in Prose*

The Famous Victories of Henry V: *A Retelling*

From the Iliad *to the* Odyssey: *A Retelling in Prose of Quintus of Smyrna's* Posthomerica

George Chapman, Ben Jonson, and John Marston's Eastward Ho! *A Retelling*

George Peele's The Arraignment of Paris: *A Retelling*

George Peele's The Battle of Alcazar: *A Retelling*

George Peele's David and Bathsheba, and the Tragedy of Absalom: *A Retelling*

George Peele's Edward I: *A Retelling*

George Peele's The Old Wives' Tale: *A Retelling*

George-a-Greene: *A Retelling*

The History of King Leir: *A Retelling*

Homer's Iliad: *A Retelling in Prose*

Homer's Odyssey: *A Retelling in Prose*

J.W. Gent.'s The Valiant Scot: *A Retelling*

Jason and the Argonauts: A Retelling in Prose of Apollonius of Rhodes' Argonautica

John Ford: Eight Plays Translated into Modern English

John Ford's The Broken Heart: *A Retelling*

John Ford's The Fancies, Chaste and Noble: *A Retelling*

John Ford's The Lady's Trial: *A Retelling*

John Ford's The Lover's Melancholy: *A Retelling*

John Ford's Love's Sacrifice: *A Retelling*

John Ford's Perkin Warbeck: *A Retelling*

John Ford's The Queen: *A Retelling*

John Ford's 'Tis Pity She's a Whore: *A Retelling*

John Lyly's Campaspe: *A Retelling*

John Lyly's Endymion, The Man in the Moon: *A Retelling*

John Lyly's Galatea: *A Retelling*

John Lyly's Love's Metamorphosis: *A Retelling*

John Lyly's Midas: *A Retelling*

John Lyly's Mother Bombie: *A Retelling*

John Lyly's Sappho and Phao: *A Retelling*

John Lyly's The Woman in the Moon: *A Retelling*

John Webster's The White Devil: *A Retelling*

King Edward III: *A Retelling*

Mankind: *A Medieval Morality Play* (A Retelling)

Margaret Cavendish's The Unnatural Tragedy: *A Retelling*

The Merry Devil of Edmonton: *A Retelling*

The Summoning of Everyman: *A Medieval Morality Play* (A Retelling)

Robert Greene's Friar Bacon and Friar Bungay: *A Retelling*

The Taming of a Shrew: *A Retelling*

Tarlton's Jests: A Retelling

Thomas Middleton's A Chaste Maid in Cheapside: *A Retelling*

Thomas Middleton's Women Beware Women: *A Retelling*

Thomas Middleton and Thomas Dekker's The Roaring Girl: *A Retelling*

Thomas Middleton and William Rowley's The Changeling: *A Retelling*

The Trojan War and Its Aftermath: Four Ancient Epic Poems

Virgil's Aeneid: *A Retelling in Prose*

William Shakespeare's 5 Late Romances: Retellings in Prose

William Shakespeare's 10 Histories: Retellings in Prose

William Shakespeare's 11 Tragedies: Retellings in Prose

William Shakespeare's 12 Comedies: Retellings in Prose

William Shakespeare's 38 Plays: Retellings in Prose

William Shakespeare's 1 Henry IV, aka Henry IV, Part 1: *A Retelling in Prose*

William Shakespeare's 2 Henry IV, aka Henry IV, Part 2: *A Retelling in Prose*

William Shakespeare's 1 Henry VI, aka Henry VI, Part 1: *A Retelling in Prose*

William Shakespeare's 2 Henry VI, aka Henry VI, Part 2: *A Retelling in Prose*

William Shakespeare's 3 Henry VI, aka Henry VI, Part 3: *A Retelling in Prose*

William Shakespeare's All's Well that Ends Well: *A Retelling in Prose*

William Shakespeare's Antony and Cleopatra: *A Retelling in Prose*

William Shakespeare's As You Like It: *A Retelling in Prose*

William Shakespeare's The Comedy of Errors: *A Retelling in Prose*

William Shakespeare's Coriolanus: *A Retelling in Prose*

William Shakespeare's Cymbeline: *A Retelling in Prose*

William Shakespeare's Hamlet: *A Retelling in Prose*

William Shakespeare's Henry V: *A Retelling in Prose*

William Shakespeare's Henry VIII: *A Retelling in Prose*

William Shakespeare's Julius Caesar: *A Retelling in Prose*

William Shakespeare's King John: *A Retelling in Prose*

William Shakespeare's King Lear: *A Retelling in Prose*

William Shakespeare's Love's Labor's Lost: *A Retelling in Prose*

William Shakespeare's Macbeth: *A Retelling in Prose*

William Shakespeare's Measure for Measure: *A Retelling in Prose*

William Shakespeare's The Merchant of Venice: *A Retelling in Prose*

William Shakespeare's The Merry Wives of Windsor: *A Retelling in Prose*

William Shakespeare's A Midsummer Night's Dream: *A Retelling in Prose*

William Shakespeare's Much Ado About Nothing: *A Retelling in Prose*

William Shakespeare's Othello: *A Retelling in Prose*

William Shakespeare's Pericles, Prince of Tyre: *A Retelling in Prose*

William Shakespeare's Richard II: *A Retelling in Prose*

William Shakespeare's Richard III: *A Retelling in Prose*

William Shakespeare's Romeo and Juliet: *A Retelling in Prose*

William Shakespeare's The Taming of the Shrew: *A Retelling in Prose*

William Shakespeare's The Tempest: *A Retelling in Prose*

William Shakespeare's Timon of Athens: *A Retelling in Prose*

William Shakespeare's Titus Andronicus: *A Retelling in Prose*

William Shakespeare's Troilus and Cressida: *A Retelling in Prose*

William Shakespeare's Twelfth Night: *A Retelling in Prose*

William Shakespeare's The Two Gentlemen of Verona: *A Retelling in Prose*

William Shakespeare's The Two Noble Kinsmen: *A Retelling in Prose*

William Shakespeare's The Winter's Tale: *A Retelling in Prose*

---

[1] Source: Sara McIntosh Wooten, *Oprah Winfrey: Talk Show Legend*, pp. 67-69.

[2] Source: Therese De Angelis, *Jodie Foster*, p. 17.

[3] Source: Kermit Schafer, *The Bedside Book of Celebrity Bloopers*, p. 87.

[4] Source: Martyn Palmer, "Javier Bardem is killing them softly." *The Times.* 15 December 2007 <http://entertainment.timesonline.co.uk/tol/arts_and_entertainment/film/article3009905.ece>.

[5] Source: William Goldman, *The Princess Bride*, p. 339.

[6] Source: Tom Powers, *Movie Monsters*, pp. 19, 31.

[7] Source: Stuart Jeffries, 'I have never been a bimbo.' *The Guardian*. 28 March 2007 <http://www.guardian.co.uk/g2/story/0,,2044261,00.html>.

[8] Source: Joe Bob Briggs, *Profoundly Disturbing: Shocking Movies That Changed History!*, p. 222.

[9] Source: Michael A. Schuman, *Halle Berry: "Beauty is Not Just Physical,"* pp. 35-36.

[10] Source: Peter Guttmacher, *Legendary Comedies*, p. 50.

[11] Source: Leonard Maltin, *The Great Movie Comedians*, p. 124.

[12] Source: H. Allen Smith, *Lost in the Horse Latitudes*, p. 99.

[13] Source: Toller Cranston, *Zero Tollerance*, pp. 201-202, 204.

[14] Source: Richard Roeper, "Stupidity on tap: Too many drinking games." *Chicago Sun-Times*. 13 June 2006 <http://www.suntimes.com/output/roeper/cst-nws-roep13.html>.

[15] Source: Boze Hadleigh, *Hollywood Gays*, p. 272.

[16] Source: William Caper, *Whoopi Goldberg: Comedian and Movie Star*, p. 59.

[17] Source: Paul D. Zimmerman and Burt Goldblatt, *The Marx Brothers at the Movies*, p. 17.

[18] Source: Edward Wagenknecht, *Seven Daughters of the Theater*, pp. 187-188.

[19] Source: Terry-Thomas, *Terry-Thomas Tells Tales*, p. 83.

[20] Source: Katherine E. Krohn, *Marilyn Monroe: Norma Jeane's Dream*, p. 101.

[21] Source: Sam Wellman, *Ben Affleck*, pp. 48-49.

[22] Source: John Miller, *Ralph Richardson*, p. 68.

[23] Source: Robert Tanitch, deviser and compiler, *Ralph Richardson: A Tribute*, p. 81.

[24] Source: Jim Emerson, "Robert Altman (1925-2006): Moments." *Chicago Sun-Times*. 21 November 2006 <http://blogs.suntimes.com/scanners/2006/11/robert_altman_19252006_moments.html>.

[25] Source: Peter Bogdanovich, *Peter Bogdanovich's Movie of the Week*, p. 3.

[26] Source: Leonard Maltin, *Movie Comedy Teams*, Introduction by Billy Martin, p. x.

[27] Source: Jessica Parker, *Great African Americans in Film*, p. 15.

[28] Source: Therese De Angelis, *Jodie Foster*, pp. 54-55.

[29] Source: Leonard Maltin, *Movie Comedy Teams*, p. 239.

[30] Source: Katherine E. Krohn, *Marilyn Monroe: Norma Jeane's Dream*, p. 67.

[31] Source: Patty Fox, *Star Style: Hollywood Legends as Fashion Icons*, pp. 81-82.

[32] Source: Leslie Halliwell, *The Filmgoer's Book of Quotes*, p. 195.

[33] Source: Roger Ebert, "The American Queen." *Chicago Sun-Times*. 30 June 2003 <http://www.suntimes.com/output/eb-feature/cst-ftr-xhepb30.html;>.

[34] Source: Marco Perella, *Adventures of a No Name Actor*, pp. 196-198.

[35] Source: Gerald Nachman, *Seriously Funny*, p. 331.

[36] Source: Andrew Hecht, *Hollywood Merry-Go-Round*, p. 172.

[37] Source: David Morgan, *Monty Python Speaks*, p. 264.

[38] Source: Joe Bob Briggs, *Profoundly Disturbing: Shocking Movies That Changed History!*, p. 222.

[39] Source: David Brown, *Star Billing: Tell-Tale Trivia from Hollywood*, p. 17.

[40] Source: Doreen Gonzales, *AIDS: Ten Stories of Courage*, pp. 17, 24-25.

[41] Source: Judith C. Galas, *Gay Rights*, p. 79.

[42] Source: Art Linkletter, *Oops!*, pp. 108-109.

[43] Source: Nancy Caldwell Sorel and Edward Sorel, *First Encounters*, p. 121.

[44] Source: Joe Adamson, *Tex Avery: King of Cartoons*, pp. 127-128.

[45] Source: Bob Hope, *The Road to Hollywood*, p. 22.

[46] Source: An A&E *Biography* program featuring Ernie Kovacs.

[47] Source: Nick Harris, *I Wish I'd Said That!*, p. 103.

[48] Source: Lore and Maurice Cowan, *The Wit of the Jews*, pp. 104-105.

[49] Source: Vincent Price, *The Book of Joe*, p. 97.

[50] Source: An interview with Jimmy Stewart that is included in the MCA video of *Harvey*.

[51] Source: Roger Ebert, *Mon Oncle*. Chicago Sun-Times. 9 June 2003 <http://suntimes.com/ebert/greatmovies/mononcle.html>.

[52] Source: Leslie Halliwell, *The Filmgoer's Book of Quotes*, p. 46.

[53] Source: Donald J. Sobol, *Encyclopedia Brown's Book of the Wacky Outdoors*, p. 77.

[54] Source: Bill Worland, "*Fumble Four Bars In*," pp. 88-89.

[55] Source: Arthur Diamond, *Charlie Chaplin*, p. 86.

[56] Source: Jessica Parker, *Great African Americans in Film*, p. 57.

[57] Source: Arthur Marx, *Life With Groucho*, pp. 175-176.

[58] Source: Candido Bonvicini, *The Tenor's Son: My Days With Pavarotti*, pp. 134-135.

[59] Source: The documentary *W.C. Fields: Straight Up*.

[60] Source: Eddie Cantor, *As I Remember Them*, p. 84.

[61] Source: Bob Thomas, *Bud & Lou*, pp. 42-43.

[62] Source: Angele de T. Gingras, *From Bussing to Bugging*, p. 73.

[63] Source: Richard Roeper, "Oscar diary: Stuff you didn't see on TV." *Chicago Sun-Times.* 7 March 2006 <http://www.suntimes.com/output/roeper/cst-nws-roep071.html>.

[64] Source: Glenhall Taylor, *Before Television*, p. 129.

[65] Source: H. Allen Smith, *Low Man on a Totem Pole*, p. 66.

[66] Source: Victoria Horne Oakie, compiler and editor, *"Dear Jack,"* front matter.

[67] Source: The documentary *W.C. Fields: Straight Up*.

[68] Source: Tomie dePaola, *26 Fairmount Avenue*, pp. 16-23.

[69] Source: Tom Powers, *Horror Movies*, p. 31.

[70] Source: Barry Took, *Comedy Greats*, p. 174.

[71] Source: Arthur Marx, *Son of Groucho*, p. 170.

[72] Source: Joe Garner, *Now Showing: Unforgettable Moments from the Movies*, pp. 29-30.

[73] Source: David Morgan, *Monty Python Speaks*, p. 250.

[74] Source: Joseph Weintraub, editor, *The Wit and Wisdom of Mae West*, p. 89.

[75] Source: Vincent Price, *The Book of Joe*, p. 93.

[76] Source: Paul D. Zimmerman and Burt Goldblatt, *The Marx Brothers at the Movies*, p. 83.

[77] Source: Laurie Stone, *Laughing in the Dark*, p. 88.

[78] Source: John A. Williams and Dennis A. Williams, *If I Stop I'll Die*, p. 126.

[79] Source: Jim Haskins and N.R. Mitgang, *Mr. Bojangles*, p. 216.

[80] Source: An interview with Jimmy Stewart that is included in the MCA video of *Harvey*.

[81] Source: Paul Parla and Charles P. Mitchell, *Screen Sirens Scream!*, pp. 117-118.

[82] Source: Jim Haskins and N.R. Mitgang, *Mr. Bojangles*, p. 231.

[83] Source: Rusty E. Frank, *Tap!*, p. 146.

[84] Source: Bruce Vilanch, *Bruce! Adventures in the Skin Trade and Other Essays*, p. 24.

[85] Source: Mary Malone, *Will Rogers: Cowboy Philosopher*, p. 95.

[86] Source: Gail Blasser Riley, *Wah Ming Chang: Artist and Master of Special Effects*, p. 11.

[87] Source: Tomie dePaola, *Things Will NEVER Be the Same*, p. 21.

[88] Source: Bart Rockwell, *World's Strangest Basketball Stories*, p. 5.

[89] Source: Robert Lewis Taylor, *W.C. Fields: His Follies and Fortunes*, pp. 314-315.

[90] Source: Bob Bernotas, *Spike Lee: Filmmaker*, p. 23.

[91] Source: Patty Fox, *Star Style: Hollywood Legends as Fashion Icons*, p. 67.

[92] Source: Bruce Nash and Allan Zullo, *The Hollywood Walk of Shame*, p. 40.

[93] Source: W.K. Martin, *Marlene Dietrich*, p. 79.

[94] Source: Michael Boo, *The Story of Figure Skating*, p. 32.

[95] Source: John Waters, *Crackpot: The Obsessions of John Waters*, pp. 51-52.

[96] Source: John Waters, *Shock Value*, p. 24.

[97] Source: Jim Emerson, "Robert Altman (1925-2006): Moments." *Chicago Sun-Times.* 21 November 2006 <http://blogs.suntimes.com/scanners/2006/11/robert_altman_19252006_moments.html>.

[98] Source: Robert Morley, *Robert Morley's Book of Bricks*, p. 40.

[99] Source: Diana Rigg, compiler, *No Turn Unstoned*, p. 179.

[100] Source: Paul Bailey, editor, *The Stately Homo: A Celebration of the Life of Quentin Crisp*, p. 208.

[101] Source: Bill Adler, *Fred Astaire: A Wonderful Life*, pp. 11-12.

[102] Source: Edward Edelson, *Funny Men of the Movies*, p. 21.

[103] Source: Sarah Giles, *Fred Astaire: His Friends Talk*, p. 192.

[104] Source: Sheldon Leonard, *And the Show Goes On*, pp. 66-67.

[105] Source: Michael Moore, *Stupid White Men*, pp. 59-60.

[106] Source: Arthur Diamond, *Charlie Chaplin*, p. 93.

[107] Source: Ron Smith, *Comic Support*, p. 14.

[108] Source: H. Allen Smith, *Lost in the Horse Latitudes*, p. 202.

[109] Source: Rabbi Joseph Telushkin, *Jewish Wisdom*, p. 257.

[110] Source: Stephen M. Silverman, *Funny Ladies*, p. 92.

[111] Source: Candace Havens, *Joss Whedon: The Genius Behind Buffy*, p. 49.

[112] Source: Eddie Cantor, *Take My Life*, p. 111.

[113] Source: Bob Hope, *The Road to Hollywood*, p. 104.

[114] Source: Peter Jacobsen, *Embedded Balls*, p. 141.

[115] Source: Edward K. Rowell, editor, *Humor for Preaching and Teaching*, p. 186.

[116] Source: Paul Parla and Charles P. Mitchell, *Screen Sirens Scream!*, p. 233.

[117] Source: Joe Garner, *Now Showing: Unforgettable Moments from the Movies*, p. 49.

[118] Source: Samuel Crowl, *Shakespeare at the Cineplex: The Kenneth Branagh Era*, pp. 129-130.

[119] Source: Luc Sante and Melissa Holbrook Pierson, editors, *O.K. You Mugs: Writers on Movie Actors*, pp. 224-225.

[120] Source: An A&E *Biography* program featuring Peter Lorre.

[121] Source: Peter Jacobsen, *Embedded Balls*, pp. 3-4.

[122] Source: Lawrence J. Epstein, *The Haunted Smile*, pp. 101-102.

[123] Source: Bob Thomas, *Bud & Lou*, pp. 40, 135.

[124] Source: Leonard Feather and Jack Tracy, *Laughter from the Hip: The Lighter Side of Jazz*, pp. 62-63.

[125] Source: Roland L. Bessette, *Mario Lanza: Tenor in Exile*, pp. 85, 174.

[126] Source: Groucho Marx, *Groucho and Me*, p. 236.

[127] Source: Michael A. Schuman, *Halle Berry: "Beauty is Not Just Physical,"* pp. 24-25, 27.

[128] Source: Joe E. Brown, *Laughter is a Wonderful Thing*, p. 5.

[129] Source: Sam Wellman, *Ben Affleck*, p. 21.

[130] Source: Lawrence J. Epstein, *Mixed Nuts*, p. 102.

[131] Source: Edward Edelson, *Funny Men of the Movies*, pp. 11, 55.

[132] Source: Roland L. Bessette, *Mario Lanza: Tenor in Exile*, p. 115.

[133] Source: Michael Boo, *The Story of Figure Skating*, p. 68.

[134] Source: Betty White, *Here We Go Again*, p. 133.

[135] Source: The documentary *The Marx Brothers in a Nutshell*.

[136] Source: Sally Kline, editor, *George Lucas: Interviews*, p. 45.

[137] Source: John Kenneth Muir, *An Askew View*, p. 13.

[138] Source: Diana Maychick, *Audrey Hepburn*, p. 58.

[139] Source: Arthur Marx, *Son of Groucho*, p. 178.

[140] Source: Jamie Griggs Tevis, *My Life with the Hustler*, pp. 196-197.

[141] Source: Kathleen Tracy, *The Girl's Got Bite*, pp. 72-74.

[142] Source: Michael Thomas Ford, *It's Not Mean If It's True*, p. 105.

[143] Source: Nancy Caldwell Sorel and Edward Sorel, *First Encounters*, p. 95.

[144] Source: Toller Cranston, *Zero Tollerance*, p. 112.

[145] Source: Michael A. Schuman, *Halle Berry: "Beauty is Not Just Physical,"* p. 55.

[146] Source: Tanaquil Le Clercq, *The Ballet Cook Book*, p. 117.

[147] Source: Lewis C. Henry, *Humorous Anecdotes About Famous People*, p. 200.

[148] Source: Robert Morley, *Around the World in Eighty-One Years*, p. 141.

[149] Source: John Waters, *Crackpot: The Obsessions of John Waters*, p. 39.

[150] Source: Kenneth Williams, *Acid Drops*, p. 17.

[151] Source: The documentary *The Marx Brothers in a Nutshell*.

[152] Source: Amy Allison, *Antonio Banderas*, pp. 32-33.

[153] Source: Robert Morley, *Robert Morley's Book of Bricks*, p. 46.

[154] Source: Bruce Campbell, *If Chins Could Kill: Confessions of a B Movie Actor*, p. 108.

[155] Source: Jay David, *The Life and Humor of Robin Williams*, p. 174.

[156] Source: An A&E *Biography* program featuring Debbie Reynolds.

[157] Source: John Kenneth Muir, *An Askew View*, p. 95.

[158] Source: Jay David, *The Life and Humor of Robin Williams*, pp. 143-144.

[159] Source: Miriam Weiss Meyer, project editor, *Top Picks: People*, pp. 67-69.

[160] Source: Tanaquil Le Clercq, *The Ballet Cook Book*, pp. 252-253.

[161] Source: Peter Guttmacher, *Legendary Comedies*, p. 33.

[162] Source: Phyllis Diller, *Like a Lampshade in a Whorehouse: My Life in Comedy*, p. 187.

[163] Source: Art Linkletter, *Oops!*, p. 64.

[164] Source: Graham Chapman, *Graham Crackers*, pp. 65-66.

[165] Source: Robert Morley, *Around the World in Eighty-One Years*, p. 81.

[166] Source: Bruce Vilanch, *Bruce! Adventures in the Skin Trade and Other Essays*, p. 14.

[167] Source: John Miller, *Ralph Richardson*, p. 122.

[168] Source: Leonard Maltin, *The Great Movie Comedians*, p. 120.

[169] Source: Lawrence J. Epstein, *Mixed Nuts*, p. 107.

[170] Source: Glenhall Taylor, *Before Television*, pp. 68, 70.

[171] Source: Lawrence J. Epstein, *The Haunted Smile*, p. 91.

[172] Source: Frank Manchel, *The Rise of Film Comedy*, p. 112.

[173] Source: Penelope Gilliatt, *Jacques Tati*, p. 10.

[174] Source: J. Bryan III, *Merry Gentlemen (and One Lady)*, p. 117.

[175] Source: Michael Bronski, consulting editor, *Outstanding Lives*, p. 376.

[176] Source: Helen Traubel, *St. Louis Woman*, p. 256.

[177] Source: Hal Burton, editor, *Acting in the Sixties*, p. 244.

[178] Source: Edward Wagenknecht, *Seven Daughters of the Theater*, p. 200.

[179] Source: Jim Tully, *A Dozen and One*, p. 141.

[180] Source: Mark Russell, editor, *Out of Character*, p. 102.

[181] Source: Grace Moore, *You're Only Human Once*, pp. 231-232.

[182] Source: D.L. Mabery, *George Lucas*, pp. 24-25.

[183] Source: Peter Bogdanovich, *Peter Bogdanovich's Movie of the Week*, pp. 116-118.

[184] Source: Rusty E. Frank, *Tap!*, p. 163.

[185] Source: Candido Bonvicini, *The Tenor's Son: My Days With Pavarotti*, p. 98.

[186] Source: Helen Traubel, *St. Louis Woman*, p. 270.

[187] Source: Michael Moore, *Stupid White Men*, pp. 97, 100.

[188] Source: Peter Hay, *Movie Anecdotes*, p. 237.

[189] Source: Groucho Marx, *Groucho and Me*, p. 323.

[190] Source: William Goldman, *The Princess Bride*, p. 328.

[191] Source: Joe Adamson, *Tex Avery: King of Cartoons*, pp. 129-130.

[192] Source: John Canemaker, *Tex Avery: The MGM Years, 1942-1955*, p. 178.

[193] Source: Amy Allison, *Antonio Banderas*, pp. 19-20.

[194] Source: H. Allen Smith, *Low Man on a Totem Pole*, p. 152.

[195] Source: Paul Bailey, editor, *The Stately Homo: A Celebration of the Life of Quentin Crisp*, pp. 157-159.

[196] Source: Ben Primack, adapter and editor, *The Ben Hecht Show*, p. 161.

[197] Source: Sheldon Leonard, *And the Show Goes On*, p. 89.

[198] Source: Eddie Cantor, *As I Remember Them*, pp. 102-104.

[199] Source: Bob Bernotas, *Spike Lee: Filmmaker*, pp. 8-10.

[200] Source: Boze Hadleigh, *Hollywood Gays*, p. 340.

[201] Source: Terry-Thomas, *Terry-Thomas Tells Tales*, p. 82.

[202] Source: Ellen Erlanger, *Jane Fonda: More Than a Movie Star*, p. 36.

[203] Source: John A. Williams and Dennis A. Williams, *If I Stop I'll Die*, p. 44.

[204] Source: Rabbi Joseph Telushkin, *Jewish Wisdom*, p. 109.

[205] Source: Ellen Erlanger, *Jane Fonda: More Than a Movie Star*, p. 30.

[206] Source: Sara McIntosh Wooten, *Oprah Winfrey: Talk Show Legend*, pp. 80-81.

[207] Source: Frank Manchel, *The Rise of Film Comedy*, p. 100.

[208] Source: Luc Sante and Melissa Holbrook Pierson, editors, *O.K. You Mugs: Writers on Movie Actors*, pp. 11-12.

[209] Source: David K. Fremon, *The Great Depression in American History*, p. 80.

[210] Source: Graham Chapman, *Graham Crackers*, p. 46.

[211] Source: Joe Hyams, *Zen in the Martial Arts*, pp. 89-90.

[212] Source: Bruce Nash and Allan Zullo, *The Hollywood Walk of Shame*, p. 41.

[213] Source: Gerald Nachman, *Seriously Funny*, p. 357.

[214] Source: John Waters, *Shock Value*, pp. 50, 52.

[215] Source: Bill Adler, *Fred Astaire: A Wonderful Life*, p. 128.

[216] Source: An A&E *Biography* program featuring Jackie Chan.

[217] Source: Geraldine Farrar, *Such Sweet Compulsion*, p. 184.

[218] Source: Sally Kline, editor, *George Lucas: Interviews*, p. 66.

[219] Source: Corey Ford, *The Time of Laughter*, p. 190.

[220] Source: Sarah Giles, *Fred Astaire: His Friends Talk*, p. 16.

[221] Source: Marco Perella, *Adventures of a No Name Actor*, pp. 128-129.

[222] Source: J. Bryan III, *Merry Gentlemen (and One Lady)*, pp. 169-170.

[223] Source: Peter Hay, *Movie Anecdotes*, p. 223.

[224] Source: Andrew Hecht, *Hollywood Merry-Go-Round*, p. 179.

[225] Source: D.L. Mabery, *George Lucas*, pp. 23-24.

[226] Source: Gail Blasser Riley, *Wah Ming Chang: Artist and Master of Special Effects*, pp. 69-72.

[227] Source: Tom Powers, *Movie Monsters*, p. 58.

[228] Source: Tom Powers, *Horror Movies*, p. 45.

[229] Source: Peggy Fleming, *The Long Program*, p. 176.

[230] Source: Steve Lipman, *Laughter in Hell*, p. 103.

[231] Source: David Brown, *Star Billing: Tell-Tale Trivia from Hollywood*, p. 34.

[232] Source: Art Linkletter, *I Wish I'd Said That!*, pp. 25-26. Also: Corey Ford, *The Time of Laughter*, p. 195.

[233] Source: Stephen M. Silverman, *Funny Ladies*, p. 49.

[234] Source: Victoria Horne Oakie, compiler and editor, *"Dear Jack,"* p. 32.

[235] Source: Phyllis Diller, *Like a Lampshade in a Whorehouse: My Life in Comedy*, p. 182.

[236] Source: Ron Smith, *Comic Support*, p. 120.

[237] Source: Laurie Stone, *Laughing in the Dark*, p. 88.

[238] Source: Joe Morella and Edward Z. Epstein, *Forever Lucy*, pp. 33-34.

[239] Source: Bruce Campbell, *If Chins Could Kill: Confessions of a B Movie Actor*, p. 229.

[240] Source: Arthur Marx, *Life With Groucho*, p. 193.

[241] Source: Kathleen Tracy, *The Girl's Got Bite*, pp. 71-72.

[242] Source: Bradley Steffens and Robyn M. Weaver, *Cartoonists*, p. 37.

[243] Source: Ben Primack, adapter and editor, *The Ben Hecht Show*, pp. 125-126.

[244] Source: Joe E. Brown, *Laughter is a Wonderful Thing*, p. 4.

[245] Source: John Canemaker, *Tex Avery: The MGM Years, 1942-1955*, p. 16.

[246] Source: Geoffrey Macnab, "Carry on flogging a dead horse." *The Guardian*. 18 May 2006 <http://www.guardian.co.uk/g2/story/0,,1777171,00.html>.

[247] Source: Miriam Weiss Meyer, project editor, *Top Picks: People*, pp. 6-7.

[248] Source: *Current Biography Yearbook*, 1985, p. 145.

[249] Source: Michael Moore, *Downsize This!*, p. 295.

[250] Source: Penelope Gilliatt, *Jacques Tati*, p. 11.

www.ingramcontent.com/pod-product-compliance
Lightning Source LLC
Chambersburg PA
CBHW060444160726

47992CB00003B/1062